GOLD Counselling®
Second Edition

*A Structured Psychotherapeutic Approach To The
Mapping And Re-Aligning Of Belief Systems*

Georges Philips
&
Lyn Buncher
with
Brian Stevenson

Foreword by Dr Sheila Cromwell

Crown House Publishing Limited
www.crownhouse.co.uk

Published in the UK by

Crown House Publishing Ltd
Crown Buildings
Bancyfelin
Carmarthen
Wales
www.crownhouse.co.uk

First published 1997
Second edition 1999
Reprinted 2000

British Library of Cataloguing-in-Publication Data
A catalogue entry for this book is available
from the British Library.

ISBN 1899836330

Printed and bound in Wales by
Gomer Press
Llandysul
Ceredigion
SA44 4QL

We dedicate this book to the spirit of life
which we know is within all of you

How to understand how your beliefs underpin
EVERY action you've EVER carried out and EVERY
feeling you've ever had… and how to revise those beliefs so as to
create your own successes.

Techniques to deal with "lies, damned lies, and beliefs".

How to understand why so many techniques that you
may have tried before did not work, and would not
ever have worked, permanently.

An advanced therapists' guidebook to applying
GOLD Counselling analysis procedures with NLP to facilitate
change in clients' lives, and in your own, permanently.

Acknowledgments

This book would not have been possible without the pioneering work of Steve and Connirae Andreas, Richard Bandler, Robert Dilts, John Grinder and other major developers of NLP.
Also Edward De Bono, Deepak Chopra and Stuart Wild who have influenced the making of this book through their work on personal development and thinking strategies.

Our thanks

…Many thanks to the many people whom we've worked with and who have made this book possible… lots of people… too numerous to mention… but with special thanks to Peter Crawford, Lyne Driscoll, Susan Ermelli, Michelle Harris, Tina Hawkins, Burt Hotchkiss, Jacquelyne Morison, Andy Parr, Vera Peiffer, Terence Watts, and Patricia Way, to name but a few.

Table of Contents

Foreword
by Dr Sheila Cromwell

It is a pleasure to read a thesis set out with such clarity, and to follow through the lucid development. The NLP field is an accretion of many ideas and strategies from different sources. Strength and interest is derived from these successive inputs. It would be a pity if rigid fossilisation should ever set in. There is always room for fresh thought.

It is therefore refreshing to discover a new system slotted in. Not that the authors claim that the system they have developed is an NLP technique. However, a time-honoured NLP pattern is apparent in that primary beliefs are intuitively accessed in a light trance state and then cognitively questioned, albeit within limits. This mixture of intuition and cognition, while characteristically NLP in concept, has been developed by the authors in *GOLD Counselling* in a system all their own – a system that stands sturdily on its own. By repetitive gentle questioning on a theme (with verbal variation), negative primary beliefs are deconstructed.

It can be said that NLP has been slotted into this process. NLP practitioners, well-versed in the ecological implications of the NLP strategies referred to in the final section, will find a useful additional tool, and one that can be used more broadly even than has been indicated.

I particularly liked the freshness of thought that questioned time-honoured concepts and presuppositions, as in "planning to fail" (page 237) and in the authors' Structural pre-suppositions 1 and 2 on page 63 and page 64.

The possible conflict of beliefs is thoughtfully approached and the dangers of seeking integration before resolution of the differences are indicated, (in a parallel way, but through a totally different strategy, to that of Robert Dilts et al. who warned of an otherwise possible disintegration of a client's thinking process, in *Beliefs*, Metamorphous Press 1990).

The outstanding merit of this book lies in the mapping. Once the client has, through a process of free-thinking in a light trance, made a list of words associated (however seemingly remotely and loosely) with the therapy topic, then, by means of mapping their connections, the client's primary beliefs with regard to that topic are derived. These maps, generously illustrated, are helpfully clear.

I think this book is a very useful addition to therapeutic practice and deserves the success I wish it.

Sheila Cromwell

*Have you ever wondered what you could
achieve if you believed, yes, you really believed,
you could **ONLY** succeed?…*

…so WHY aren't you doing it, right now?

Preface

Everything that we ever say or do starts from an idea which we think.

How often have you heard people say things like, *"You can't teach an old dog new tricks"*, or perhaps, *"No, I can't do that. Tried it once and failed."* Another regularly used phrase is *"I have to, but, I can't"*.

Well, if these phrases ring any bells with you, you're not alone. We have used these words too. Even now as we enter the twenty-first century with all the possibilities we have around us, why is it that so many people live lives that are but a pale imitation of the lives which they could really live? It's just that they don't believe that they could achieve that which they want.

During the last few years, significant advances have been made in the understandings of how we think and operate within the world. From these advances, it has been possible to develop a new way of thinking to become aware of the ideas, values and beliefs which are stored within each of us.

By integrating these new understandings, it has been possible to create an approach which permits us to effectively "see inside" another person's mind and to remove or redesign any of the limitations which are stored in there. In addition, it is a methodology that allows a client to accurately design a belief system that fulfils their expectation of life. The techniques which we have developed to enable this to take place are known as GOLD Counselling. This approach is, quite simply, the most powerful, most efficient and most effective way to restructure beliefs yet devised.

At this point a word of caution is called for. As you continue to read further into this book, you will find certain comments, which may appear impossible or perhaps implausible. Yes, some do sound strange. Yes, some do feel impossible. Yes, some appear to go against considered wisdom. And, yes, they are all true.

Once you have grasped the essence of what GOLD Counselling is, you will understand more about the unconscious mind than most therapists of whatever school anywhere in the world. We know the techniques work. We understand why they work. And we can prove they work. We have found them to facilitate *permanent* success with our clients, time and time again.

Many of you reading this book will already be either competent in Neuro-Linguistic Programming (NLP), or undergoing training in that field. We have found that the skills available to NLP Practitioners at whatever level are significant life-enhancing tools. However, these tools do not as yet integrate the specific new learnings, which have been identified. It is by applying these new learnings which you will find presented in this book that you will be able to truly understand, possibly for the very first time, why so many people fail to achieve those things which they believe they really want in life.

We strongly recommend, to those who intend to use GOLD Counselling in the field of personal therapy, to attend a GOLD Counsellor's practitioner's workshop/training weekend as it is not possible to transmit in the written form some of the more subtle nuances that are available within GOLD Counselling.

How this book is structured

Within Section One of this book we have set out an explanation of how the mind operates using its beliefs, and how each of these beliefs connects to other beliefs, be they liberating or restricting. We then explain exactly how permanent and self-perpetuating these beliefs are. Once installed, whatever that person does will always be filtered through these beliefs on an unconscious level.

You will learn and find explanations as to how the mind uses energy to fulfil beliefs, why it is that we all seem to hold apparently conflicting beliefs and how it is possible to experience such things as elation one minute and depression the next.

Section Two of this book contains the key elements which you must understand so that you can appreciate what GOLD Counselling is and how it works. The first chapter in Section Two gives an explanation of why positive thinking is not able to create change on a permanent basis. You will find an explanation of how this method of counselling can be applied to identify and eliminate limiting beliefs. Once this elimination has taken place, a person will then be able to naturally and effortlessly take himself forward towards the success which he desires in a congruent and focused manner.

Throughout this Section we have incorporated examples to highlight and focus awareness on the specific issues being raised. Actual case studies are included which elaborate further the process of GOLD Counselling. By reference to these examples, we would expect a therapist to gain a deeper understanding of how this process works and realise the speed, power and accuracy of the techniques within this book.

Section Three contains actual client case studies. This section is structured so that the examples become progressively more complex and involved, showing you the breadth of presenting problems which can be effectively worked through with these techniques.

Section Four is structured so that people with a working knowledge of NLP will be able to appreciate how the GOLD Counselling approach can be used in conjunction with specific NLP techniques. Each chapter contains context-specific examples in order to identify how these would occur in a therapeutic situation. The NLP techniques discussed include such procedures as Swish, Six-Step Reframes, New-Behaviour Generators and well-formed outcomes.

When you study this section you will realise that at all times we thoroughly endorse the existing NLP techniques. Where we find a synergetic overlap is in using the GOLD Counselling approach in order to identify and work through the underlying cause, rather than just working with the symptom. Once carried out, if additional techniques are required these can then be applied to the correct place in the client's map of experiences.

Section Five is dedicated to specific strategies that have been developed by independent GOLD Practitioners. It allows individuals to contribute material which incorporates the GOLD Model in the areas of therapy or personal development.

If you have developed a strategy that may benefit other therapists and wish to make a contribution, please contact the authors.

If you are an NLP Practitioner of whatever level, beginner, intermediate or advanced, GOLD Counselling will expose you to the possibility of so many more successes than you could have ever imagined before.

We have taught these techniques to NLP Practitioners who have then gone on to significantly improve the quality of their work.

Section One:

How The Mind Works

Introduction to Section One

Within this section we have set out how the mind operates and explained how the two separate parts, the conscious mind and the unconscious mind, relate to each other. You will find an explanation of the way in which memory, energy and words are used within the mind and how the unconscious mind sorts and categorises every belief you have ever held.

1. A Metaphor For The Mind

It has been said that however well someone is trained to drive a car or ride a motorbike, one of the greatest ways of differentiating one person's competency from another is to notice how much feel they have for the machine they are operating. Perhaps you've been in a car with someone who habitually revs the engine up to the maximum every time before changing up a gear, someone who accelerates hard towards the red light ahead and, at the last minute, slams on the brakes.

Or perhaps, going to the other extreme, someone who is over-cautious, so timid and unwilling to use the power within the machine that he actually seems to create that accident which he fears so much. Whereas if someone, while learning how to drive a car or ride a motorbike, is also taught how the actual machinery works, then he would have a better feel for it and would be that much more able to stay in control. This shows up in situations when unexpected occurrences take place, such as driving over a patch of black ice and then losing control of the direction of travel.

In the same way, we all have within us a brain of awesome power and potential, but no training was ever given or any user's manual supplied.

This wouldn't be so bad if, like those engines in the cars and motorbikes, we could take our brains apart and look inside to understand how it all works, but, unfortunately, it's not as simple as that. Notwithstanding all the scientific research which has been applied to the brain and its thinking patterns, no-one can explain scientifically how it actually works.

Furthermore, whenever we are unhappy with life or feel disease (spelt *dis-ease*), or infection (spelt *in-fection*), we are experiencing the anomalies that we create between what we believe to be true and what is true. Since the only reference point within our unconscious mind is what the unconscious mind believes to be real, whenever we feel good or bad or indifferent about an incident, it must be because of the way thoughts have been stored and coded within our mind. And this thought has, in turn, led to the creation of a belief about the world or life or a particular facet thereof.

To elaborate further, consider the following. Medical research has proven that if one group of patients is given a specific drug to speed up their heartbeat, a second group given a drug to slow their heartbeat and a third group administered a placebo, a neutral-effect substance, then the following is known to occur: whatever the patients are told will be caused by the drug *will* occur within them. If the people given the placebo are told that they will find their heartbeat increasing and they believe it, then it will happen. And if people are given a drug to increase their heartbeat, but advised that the drug will slow it down, then, if they believe it, their heartbeat will actually slow down.

2. *What Are Thoughts And Beliefs?*

2.1 Where do beliefs originate?

Let us assume for a moment that a client visits you to gain assistance in increasing his confidence. If you were to start the process by asking him about what may be stopping him from having confidence, he would probably respond with comments about feelings of or memories of past lapses in confidence or such like. Perhaps in some cases he would not be able to be so specific. It may be just a general feeling which he has that stops him.

If he did have any memories to explain why he was not confident, then each of these individual thoughts will have become justifying reasons why he believes this is so. These explanations could take the shape of many different thoughts and memories. Perhaps he was bullied at school, perhaps he didn't feel he had any role models, or perhaps he may have confused confidence with aggression, or perhaps he doesn't feel he deserves the things confidence will bring, and so on. Each of these thoughts must have originated at a certain time in his life and will have been generated from a wide variety of sources.

All of these thoughts combine together to create a belief which has been formed by that person's experience. As therapists in the present we don't know, and possibly may never know, whether that person's experience was real or imagined, or whether his interpretation was true or false. However, we can be certain that on that particular day, at that particular time in the past, that person interpreted his thoughts in a certain way and from those thoughts a belief was created, a belief as to what that thought meant to him.

Once an interpretation or belief has been given to a thought, it then becomes a reference point to enable that person to understand the world and, at the same time, it becomes part of a structure that the unconscious mind will use to filter and sort all subsequent thoughts.

Naturally, this method of using beliefs to filter and sort new thoughts will create more thoughts of a similar belief. Take, for example, the injunction *"Don't think of pink elephants."* How many of you, when filtering your minds with that injunction would be able to see nothing except pink elephants? Beliefs, in simple terms, operate in a similar way.

A belief is formed from the way in which we interpret an experience – beliefs are created from our thoughts. An experience is any thought on which our mind dwells, even for a split second. We have hundreds of thousands of thoughts every day and these can and do originate from a variety of sources. These include but are not limited to:

- comments by friends or family addressed to us
- comments by friends or family not meant for us but overheard by us
- other people's interpretation of why events have occurred
- our interpretation of meaning to someone else's actions
- peer-group or role-model pressure
- name-calling by other children
- feelings
- books read – including poetry and religious texts
- imagined happenings, daydreams, nightdreams
- fairy-stories and fantasy-stories
- fantasy or imagination
- television, film, radio
- theatre or art
- music
- cultural background
- political parties

It can be seen from this list that there are many different routes by which a belief can be formed. Let us use an example to clarify this further. Suppose a child grows up always hearing his mother complaining about his father's aggressive attitude towards her and how he never takes her out. As he grows up, he may forget about all the times when mother told him about his father. However, he may unconsciously seek to repeat his father's way of behaving since this is how his mother and father acted and they were his role-models. He could also unconsciously imitate his mother but it is possible that the child will grow to be like the parent who showed the least amount of love. Until he is able to identify where his way of behaving came from and recognise that it was his parent's belief – and not his own – he will not be able to permanently change it.

While growing up, in childhood, there exist hundreds of thousands of separate opportunities for us to learn. From these learnings it is also possible for us to develop beliefs as to how things are, how the world is and how people (including ourselves) should behave. This means that for most people the majority of the beliefs they hold as adults will have been formed during their childhood years, often modelled from other adults such as parents or teachers.

A thought is never free-floating on its own within our mind, it will always attract and attach itself to another thought, just as every cell is attached to another cell. In this way ideas and beliefs build up and grow in strength. Each thought we have is filtered through our unconscious mind and, depending on the interpretation that it makes of the event, the thought is used to support a particular belief structure. This interpretation is always based on the level of emotional content within the experience. As an example, consider a child who feels that she does not get taken out by her mother as much as other children. If this feeling is important to her – that is, dwelled on by the unconscious mind – this will be used to form part of her belief about life. This could mean that she does not deserve to go out much or perhaps, the opposite, that she should always be going out. Whatever the belief, we can be certain that the original thought will have influenced it.

The method by which beliefs are learned can be expressed as one of SEE – DO. As children, before we can speak or interpret, we can watch and copy. We learn to grow up by copying what we see others do. As children we cannot rationalise or justify, we just experience without interpretation everything that goes on around us. It is in noticing the subtle changes and variations in voice expression and closeness shown by parents that the first beliefs in our childhood years are formed. These learnings are then integrated by our unconscious mind with other thoughts and are used as building blocks with which to construct further beliefs.

> *Our beliefs – including those which were not ours to start with – control who we are now and for evermore.*

Consider the children's catch-phrase:

> *Sticks and stones can break my bones but names can never hurt me.*

Whoever first said that had obviously never been insulted by someone about whom he cared! Words once uttered can never be forgotten. We can apologise or correct the meaning but the first message stays in place with subsequent comments. Bones repair, houses can be rebuilt but words, once said, can never be retrieved. They can have the long-term effects which are much deadlier than any artillery barrage.

It is important to note that it is not possible to determine in advance how someone will have interpreted an original event. Parents may remember events significantly differently compared to their children. However, we do know that based on the interpretation of this first event, other events will be filtered and shaped to fit in with the earlier interpretation. This is because the unconscious mind does not understand the concept of right or wrong. It does not know what positive or negative beliefs are. Take two people sitting next to each other on the train. If one were to hold a belief that LIFE IS DANGEROUS, then the unconscious mind will use this as a filter to let him experience the whole world in this way and he will probably be watching all the other passengers for the onset of danger. However, the other person may believe I'M A FRIENDLY GUY and sees in the other passengers easy-going people. This is how people can experience the same event and interpret it so differently.

2.2 Beliefs are created from thoughts

If we reconsider the client without confidence, given enough time you could continue to ask the question "Why?" to this person until you had identified all the different thoughts which he holds which are in turn the reasons why he considers himself to be without confidence. However, the actual list of thoughts could run into hundreds if the issue were very profound and important to him.

As you continue to read this book you will learn techniques to enable you to focus your client's unconscious mind so that a simplified list of the main thoughts which comprise your client's beliefs can be formed in a very short time.

It is from these individual thoughts that a belief about something is formed. Once formed, other thoughts will attach themselves to one or more of the existing beliefs within the unconscious mind and serve to reinforce the original belief.

Compare this for a moment with a game of patience. Consider how, when playing a game of patience, once the initial base cards have been dealt (equivalent to a child's first thoughts and beliefs), all other cards are required to be played in a manner which connects with those already laid down. These are the rules of the game, only certain moves (or connections) are valid in the game (equivalent to the unconscious mind).

Within the unconscious mind, a thought will never be free-floating on its own, it will always attach itself to another thought. The unconscious mind will sift and sort through all the thoughts that we have and then collate these in certain ways, often with one thought having more than one other thought connecting to it.

I am sure that most people reading this book will have at some stage in their lives looked at a railway train map. Or perhaps the map of the London Underground lines. Consider in these contexts how each line connects to another line, sometimes overlapping, sometimes ending. However, each station (belief) is in turn connected to another. No stations are left unconnected, or else no train would be able to travel along the track, and some stations are the main terminus points, at the centre of many lines.

In the same way, every belief within our mind will always need to be connected to another belief. Technical reasons will be given later but, for now, accept that this is true. You will find clear explanations as your reading progresses.

2.3 What is a belief?

In the English Oxford Dictionary you will find that a belief is defined as follows:

belief n.:
1. *The mental action, condition, or habit, of trusting to or confiding in a person or thing; trust, dependence, reliance, confidence, faith.*

2. *Mental acceptance of a proposition, statement, or fact, as true, on the ground of authority or evidence; assent of the mind to a statement, or to the truth of a fact beyond observation, on the testimony of another, or to the fact or truth on the evidence of consciousness; the mental condition involved in this assent.*

3. *The thing believed; the proposition or set of propositions held true; opinion, persuasion.*

4. *A formal statement of doctrines believed, a creed.*

5. *Confident anticipation, expectation.*

Many of the beliefs which you or your clients have will be found to be self-evident. That is, the thoughts which have created the beliefs will have been installed in recent years. However, there will often be cases when, because the originating thoughts were formed many years ago, you may well have forgotten these and consigned them to the lower reaches of your unconscious mind.

However, what happens when the dictionary is out of date, or is a translation from a foreign language and someone has made a mistake? Or if someone, by accident or on purpose, has placed the wrong definitions against the wrong words?

When people think of beliefs, they normally think of the things that they absolutely know to be true. Beliefs are felt to be opinions backed up with a certainty of truth. These are the areas of life on which we can depend, those things which we are confident are true, those things which we always expect to happen and those things which we know will occur every time.

Taking this a step further, if you were to ask a random sample of people to tell you of something they believed in and something which was important to them, you would probably be offered a variety of suggestions. These could include things such as:

The sun will rise tomorrow.
Life's hard.
The world's a friendly place.
It's a dog-eat-dog world out there.

If we were to then ask this same sample of people if this was the way in which they experienced the world, each would say YES. It is as if we find what we believe and we believe what we find. This is expressed in the *Law of Belief* which states:

> Whatever I believe my mind will always achieve for me either in reality or through my imagination in fantasy.

The mind will always find a way to fulfil the beliefs we hold. If it can do so in reality – for example, LIFE'S HARD – then it will do so by ensuring that we find things hard to do. However, if we are in an unpleasant situation, it will enable us to escape into a fantasy world in our own unconscious mind, where we can create the happiness we want in the real world.

From our own experiences and interactions with others, we all know that most people hold such beliefs about many different facets of their lives. It certainly appears that we all need beliefs to make sense of the world on a day-to-day basis and to simplify the way in which we carry on our lives. This use of beliefs gives us stability.

However, if you were to then ask our random sample of people where their beliefs came from, they would probably be quite troubled by the question. Very few people actually stop to consider where the beliefs that they hold came from. And why should they? Since a belief is something we are certain of, why double-check it? If we always did this, then surely we would all end up double-checking everything, similar to a person who compulsively checks door-locks and loses out so much in the enjoyment of life?

3. How Beliefs Are Formed

3.1 Our childhood years

During our early developmental childhood years we are in a very precarious position. On the one hand we will give total and unconditional love to our key role models (usually our mother and father) and will do whatever we can to keep them happy. Whereas, on the other hand, we haven't as yet learned whether that which they want us to be, say or do is fair or right or appropriate.

This means that we will often unwittingly accept certain ways of thinking or behaving as absolute and correct. This can and does significantly limit our development as we grow up. While in this developmental period, we are collecting and sifting information at a prodigious rate. As children we are fascinated by this new world which we have only recently entered. Every day is new, special and different. Everything we see, feel, hear, smell and taste is accepted absolutely and without any filters of questioning at all.

In addition to this external sensory input, we can also imagine from within certain things. Now it's not important whether you can't or whether you can imagine some of those early memories but you can know that they are still there, somewhere in the inner reaches of your unconscious mind.

3.2 We start making assumptions from an early age

Consider for a moment the scenario of a baby who, quite naturally and automatically, without thinking, cries when he is hungry or wants his nappy changed. Let us assume for a moment that the baby's mother became increasingly angry with the amount of crying that the baby did and felt anger towards the baby because of his crying. While the baby would not consciously understand what the feeling from his mother was, the baby would begin to experience the anger being directed towards him. This feeling of anger would create fear in the baby and the baby, naturally confused by this, would then begin to believe that he should not signal to have his needs met, since this upsets mummy and a little baby knows to do whatever it takes not to upset mummy.

Since this would be a very early and upsetting memory, it would probably be forgotten by the child as he grows up. However, this incident was so powerful that the child would create a belief about not expressing the feelings associated with needing something. This would continue to affect his personality in the present.

3.3 We accept what we are told as true

In the same way, as we grow up and venture out into the world outside the safety of our parents' home we continue to accept information in an unquestioning manner. This applies to all information received, whether positive and negative. Consider for a moment how children usually learn, by rote, automatically and without thinking. This is the way that children take in information, automatically, believing naively all that is said to them.

While all of this information is being received, there have been no mechanisms or procedures developed within our minds to answer such questions as, *"Is this right?"*, or *"Is this true?"* or, *"Is this fair?"*. As children we have not learned how to criticise, either constructively or destructively, and therefore we automatically accept EVERYTHING that is suggested to us.

This can be summarised in the phrase below:

> **"I never get what I want unless what I want is what I am. I am what I think and, therefore, I am my thoughts."**

This is a controlled programme that we all have stored within our unconscious minds and this can be, in turn, expressed as follows:

> **...I am, what I think I am, I am, what I think, I am...**

Consider for a moment the following questions:

- Did you as a child believe in Father Christmas?

- Did you believe that when you lost a tooth, fairies would place a coin under your pillow while you slept?

- Did you ever believe that life would never be the same again for you when your favourite group split up?

- Did you ever believe, at least for a while, that if you said you hated your aunt/uncle, they would never love you again?

- Did you ever believe that, because of an argument with him or her, your best friend would never ever play with you again?

It is while we, as children, are in this very sensitive and delicate phase of our development that we all have many things suggested to us. Each one of these messages, suggestions, imagined responses and comments become connected to other previously-accepted memories and are all stored away in the unconscious mind.

It is worthwhile acknowledging once again where the majority of our formative beliefs come from – our parents. They will, in turn, have received their childhood beliefs from their parents. Imagine for a moment what happens to the small child when his father, who was poorly treated by his parents (but has repressed this), treats his son in a similar cold and unfeeling manner. Naturally the child will become discomforted but he will also accept that this is the right way to behave.

3.4 An analogy

It's like Dad giving Son a disk for his computer and telling him that all the information on it is correct, up-to-date and usable. Dad believes it. So Son believes it. But Dad's been carrying that disk of data around for a long time. He's never checked to see whether new programs exist which can operate smoother or better or are perhaps more user-friendly. Perhaps he didn't know about, or didn't even bother to check whether the disk contained a computer virus. Son doesn't know where the disk came from.

(Perhaps it was from a dud batch, perhaps stolen, perhaps damaged.)

We've all heard of computer viruses, those programs which attach themselves covertly to other programs and slowly eat away at the fabric of our computer's memory and capabilities. Well, often people just don't realise that they are installing these inappropriate viruses since they don't have a way of seeing them. Perhaps they've decided to upload a massive chunk of information and hidden in there is a real stinker of a file. But since they trust the person that they've obtained the data from... well, they would never expect this to happen.

And what is also possible is that the person from whom this important and powerful information was taken didn't realise that what they were offering was corrupt. So they may continue to spread this information, without realising that it is full of hidden flaws, flaws that would slowly begin to impact on and reduce the quality of life for those in receipt.

3.5 The ego

It is astounding to consider that we all have inside us hundreds, perhaps thousands, of different beliefs, each one generated from individual thoughts. Many of these are no doubt quite different from those held dear by other people, friends and family. One must then ask, what keeps all these beliefs in place for us and ensures that they stay in force, unchanged by the influence of other people?

Within our unconscious mind the name given to the total of all the different beliefs we hold as true is **the ego.** It is our ego which embodies all that we believe about ourselves and the world. It is the ego which automatically chooses for us how to think, act and behave in any situation. It is the sum total of all our beliefs which come together to form the person we all call "I". Whenever we say something such as:

I believe.
I know it's true.
You don't care how I feel.

here we are expressing what our ego believes is true.

Often we will not know where or when the way we are feeling now first originated. All we can be sure of is that it is based on our unconscious mind's interpretation of an event, quite probably unrelated to the situation occurring now. However, we can also be sure that there was an emotional experience in that past event which was strong enough to create a permanent thought, a thought which has led to the formation of a belief – a belief which is now part of our ego.

Depending on the collection of beliefs installed within the ego, one experiences the world in a particular way. The ego acts in a similar way to a satellite-receiving dish which lets one see whatever one needs to see out there in the world so that all beliefs continue to be proven as true.

From this it follows that we are the way we are because of our beliefs, and in our lives we only notice what we receive after it has been filtered through our belief systems. When we are able to change our beliefs it then becomes possible to change how we experience the world.

> **Your ego will not let you see what does not fit in with what you already believe to be true.**

This is why people often have what appears to be so much trouble in accepting a new point of view. The mechanism which they are using to accept into their unconscious mind the new information is precisely the mechanism which needs to be changed. It is like asking one person to decide whether he personally or, alternatively, someone else with whom he works should be sacked. Self-preservation overrides everything and it keeps the status quo intact.

3.6 Projection – we are what we see in others

We have explained how everyone experiences the world via the filtering system known as their beliefs and that these are controlled by the ego. By expanding on this understanding we have shown how these beliefs will cause each of us to see the world differently, in a way which correlates with our own belief systems.

Whatever we perceive in a situation is not strictly true. It is a reflection of the beliefs of the person doing the perceiving in any given situation. If we have learned to do things in a certain way in order to gain attention or love or the absence of pain, we will naturally aim to continue acting in this way. Conversely, where we have learned to believe that some actions are painful or harmful, we will shy away from them.

Our unconscious mind has stored away within itself all the thoughts which support the beliefs we hold and each one of these thoughts has various emotions attached to it. Whenever we experience something in the here and now, we are, therefore, experiencing this through an old filter which still has old emotions attached to it. This means that the emotions which we experience in a situation now are often the emotions tied up with the original thoughts from the time when the belief was first created.

How we experience something is not a fact. It is always a reflection of the beliefs of the person perceiving the event. The situation we are experiencing is acting as a mirror-image of our emotional balance and that which we believe we see in it is, in fact, within us. Once we have changed our beliefs about what a situation means, the emotional connection we have with that incident will also change. However, until one is ready to consider the possibility of change, it will not be possible to see the situation in any other way.

What must happen is that your unconscious mind must be guided back to the time when the original belief was installed. By acting on this first thought, it is possible to change the emotional meaning of this and all future experiences.

When people use phrases similar to:

You're making me feel angry.
That's so unfair.
This is so hard.

they are filtering the world through specific beliefs of anger, unfairness and hardness respectively. Once the beliefs which support these feelings have been revised, it is then possible for people to experience the world in a totally different and more enjoyable way.

Most people seem to enjoy the company of people who have similar attitudes, aspirations and ways of behaving. This can often be seen in companies where the people who rise through the ranks are very similar to those already in those ranks.

This unconscious mirroring occurs because we all have a natural tendency to notice in others the specific characteristics which we prize in ourselves. The opposite to this also applies. It is the personality traits in others which we dislike or find uncomfortable which are in reality within us and we are seeing them in others because we are not yet ready to accept them in ourselves. Often we may say things like:

Everything would be so much easier if you were more friendly.
You're too tense.
Why don't you listen more?

This projection can be seen in the client who comes for help to deal with a particular problem which he keeps on noticing in others. The actual place where the problem is would be within his own unconscious mind and this is where we must work to effect a change. Since he, however, is not yet able to recognise the problem in himself, what is required is a method-ology which will permit the truth to be brought forth from his own uncon-scious mind.

3.7 The Law of Belief

Within the unconscious mind there exists an operating system which governs how every one of our thoughts and situations is collated and combined with those already present. This law is known as **The Law of Belief.**

The Law of Belief is a natural law which states that whatever I believe my mind always achieves for me either in reality or with my imagination as fantasy.

In addition, as children we have, naturally, a childlike innocence which means we are capable of amazing levels of imagination and a naive way of believing absolutely what we are told or what we hear or what we perceive. It is only later on as we grow up that we learn to ask questions in order to interpret with clarity the situations around us.

Consider how much more effective your reasoning abilities would have been as a child if you could have asked these types of questions at key times in your life:

- Is this right?
- Should I feel guilty?
- Why do I feel that I am to blame?
- Do my parents love me, or do they love what I do?
- Do my parents not love me, or is it only that they don't love what I do?
- Do they really care about me?
- Are they fair?
- Are they manipulating me?
- Why do they do this to me if they say they love me?
- Who are they really trying to protect – me or themselves?

This inability to interpret clearly means that we will take on messages from other people without thinking that they may be manipulating us or emotionally abusing us. This in turn causes us as children to develop beliefs about how other people will treat us.

This chain-reaction effect can be summarised as:

...thoughts give birth to ideas, which give birth to new thoughts, which give birth to new ideas...

Once a thought has been thought it can never be unthought. Thought can, however, be reviewed and altered and perceived in a different way.

The effects of this chain-reaction can be seen in clients who have had very domineering parents and who then go on to develop symptoms such as a lack of confidence. During initial questioning it will usually be found that while they do find most people bossy or domineering, they also EXPECT people to be like this. Until this chain of expectation leading to results is broken, they will continue to expect this and, naturally, this is what will happen in many of their interactions.

4. How Beliefs Are Organised Within The Mind

4.1 Overview

As discussed in Chapter 3, thoughts, ideas and images come into our minds from a myriad of sources. Once these have been accepted into our unconscious mind, the mind simplifies each of these records by carrying out a process similar to the process used to create the synopsis for a book.

Think for a moment about what a synopsis is intended to give you. It aims to sum up and condense in an abridged form the overall meaning and message of the book. From the synopsis, provided it has been worded correctly, one should be able to understand the writer's viewpoint and the ideas which he wants to put across.

4.2 The mind always aims to simplify

This is similar to the way in which the mind operates. Each thought is processed and once the synopsis has been created, it is automatically and in an instant connected to other thoughts related to similar subjects. It is from this framework of combined thoughts that beliefs are formed. The reason the mind operates in this way is because it simplifies everything. Rather than have to re-evaluate every situation to understand what it means now, it files every experience it has ever received in a simplified manner, and assumes that it means the same now as it did in the past.

Let us take the example of a girl who was to become so upset and distraught when, after an argument over a toy, her best friend said, *"If you don't let me have what I want, I'll never be your friend again"*. Feeling emotionally confused over what to do, she could have become compelled to give in to her friend's threat. As time progressed, she could connect to this belief other similarly-coded instances, each containing a theme such as, *"I must do what others want, even if I don't feel it's right or fair."*

Following the acceptance of the belief by the unconscious mind, the unconscious mind will then use this belief structure to assist it in assimilating further information. This is quite sensible since having already simplified many memories under the same heading of a belief, it can now use the belief to sift and sort additional thoughts and sensory inputs as they arise. However, once the belief is created it in turn becomes a mechanism to be used by the unconscious mind to sort and categorise further thoughts and sensory inputs.

Our teachings from NLP mean we should all be aware that billions of cellular activities are taking place within our bodies every second and that in consequence the unconscious mind will aim to simplify as much as possible through the development of belief structures. This is defined within NLP as the processes of Distortion, Deletion and Generalisation (Bandler & Grinder, 1975).

Furthermore, once the framework is in place, the unconscious mind will fight to keep it there, since to change it could well mean a drastic revision of the interpretation it has placed (remember the book synopsis) on many memories. Especially when one considers how long the belief may have been in place and since that time experiences will have occurred which corroborate the belief.

4.3 Sources of influence

A further element in the equation is from whom it was that those original beliefs were generated. This is usually, though not always, parents, teachers, other members of the family or other significant role models. The high regard in which we held these people, or perhaps the revulsion which we felt towards them, will dictate how easy it is to change the beliefs once installed. Sometimes, the people which we held in the highest regard are those which we later find out are those which influenced us the most detrimentally. Other sources of beliefs can be cartoons, magazines, films or even games we play at school.

It is important to acknowledge that during your formative years, every-thing can and may well influence you as a child. Positive incidents will influence you, negative incidents will influence you, and also things that you may feel ambivalent about will influence you. This last category is very important, since these areas of your experience that you have chosen to become neutral about may contain painful learning.

As an example, consider how a boy would feel if he were repeatedly let down by his father who keeps "forgetting" to make the time to watch him play football at school. Of course the reasons would be valid enough to the father – business trips or meetings and so on – and the son may well accept these reasons. However, this son, as he grows up to become a father, could well develop an attitude of mind whereby he is quite casual about his children's sports events, since this allows him to cover over the pain he felt as a young boy.

4.4 Primary Beliefs and Secondary Beliefs

Once a belief structure has been created within the mind, it will seek out and attach itself to other beliefs – those which are most appropriate to the underlying message contained within the original belief. It will seek out within the mind other beliefs with which it will have some affinity or similarity. Once this happens these beliefs will join together, forming a belief complex, which will, in turn, seek out other beliefs to bond with.

This ongoing procedure of beliefs seeking to bond with like beliefs which in turn look for further beliefs, can be analogised with the way in which a cancerous tumour will grow at an exponential rate and can destroy in a short time unless drastic action is taken. Or how an antidote, if administered in time, will destroy the most poisonous chemicals that may have been inadvertently introduced into the body.

This is a natural and eminently practical thing for the unconscious mind to do. This process means the unconscious mind is always simplifying and sorting itself and its surroundings to reduce the number of processes it needs to carry out.

The unconscious mind further simplifies its procedures by sorting beliefs into primary beliefs and secondary beliefs. Primary beliefs are the main beliefs, those which actually underpin the whole belief structure. These are usually the memories with the greatest emotional weight and usually, although not always, the oldest.

As an example, let us use the case of a man in his forties, single and with a weight problem. We have asked him to prepare a list for us on the beliefs he has on weight. (The process to obtain this information is clarified in Section Two).

He writes down the following items:

A Scared of food

B Fear at dinner

C Fat

D Conversation

E Ugly

F Permission

G Grown-ups

H Spots

When asked to connect these beliefs together, the following structure was obtained:

A Scared of food   **B**

B Fear at dinner   **A**

C Fat   A

D Conversation   G

E Ugly   A

F Permission   D

G Grown ups   B

H Spots   D

This can be seen when one presents his thoughts about weight in a pictorial format as a GOLD Counselling belief map.

Weight

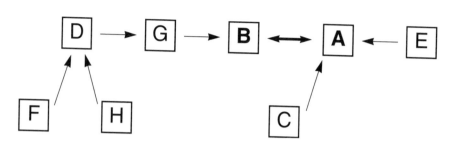

Without having to identify where his beliefs about weight were formed we already know from this that his two primary beliefs are **A** and **B**. His secondary beliefs (or lower order beliefs) all are in place to support these. Once his primary beliefs are revised, the whole of his beliefs about weight will be affected.

5. *The Theory Of Dual Or Multiple States*

5.1 Everything has at least two states of being

Within this chapter we have set out the most important elements which have been brought together to create GOLD Counselling. We have incorporated herein the specific understandings of which you will be required to develop an awareness if you are to become successful as a GOLD Counsellor. This element is the concept that we are always switching states, or emotions. One of the iron laws of nature is that everything can be in one of two states. However thinly you divide an object, there are always two sides to it. It can be night or day. A tide flows in or out. Someone may feel happy or sad.

To take a physical example, consider the method by which we use our eyes to see. Even when we focus on one point, our eyes are still moving, left-right, up-down, assessing the situation. These movements, known as saccadic movements, are essential to the proper functioning of vision. Without these regular small movements we could not take in visual information.

Another example is breathing. You cannot breathe out and in at the same time. The operating system does not permit this. Even pain is not constant. If you were to ask a patient or a doctor to describe pain he will use many different definitions and words to fine-tune the experience, but all will agree that it comes and goes, that it gets stronger then weaker. I am sure that you have been in a condition with a pain that was troubling you but after a while it just seemed to disappear. Later, however, it returned, back to the original strength.

5.2 Emotions change constantly

Within the unconscious mind, in exactly the same way, a thought will never exist on its own; each thought will always be connected to another thought within the belief structure. The rationale behind the way in which the unconscious mind sorts information is very important. Every belief structure will contain two or more beliefs, all of which are structured according to their level of *emotional* content.

In order to clarify this important point further, let us now consider the example of someone who was asked to list all the different things he feels that he does. Let us assume that a list of activities was generated as follows:

Work, Play, Eat, Drink, Fight, Make love, Sulk, Visit parents, Drive, Teach children, Cook, Travel, Sleep, Wash.

From reviewing this list, we can assume certain things. One thing is that it is unlikely that someone would be carrying out all of these activities at the same time. Therefore, he will need to swap roles or states as required. Perhaps he could be working and, at the same time, eating, drinking or travelling. However, he could not work while visiting parents. Neither could he carry out any of the former states while sleeping.

If we now take this idea a step further, let us generate a list of possible emotional states that one could enter. One possible list could appear as follows:

Happy, Sad, Aroused, Dejected, Sleepy, Bored, Jolly, Angry, Passionate, Melancholic, Delighted, Sentimental, Thrilled, Upset, Elated, and Lonely.

Most people will have experienced some or all of these states in the past. When we review the list we can see that the different states can be divided into two distinct groups as follows:

Happy	Sad
Aroused	Dejected
Sleepy	Bored
Jolly	Angry
Passionate	Melancholic
Delighted	Sentimental
Thrilled	Upset
Elated	Lonely

While we acknowledge that the above division of emotions is arbitrary, we would suggest that there are clearly certain emotions which are positive and others which are negative.

If we elaborate further, one would not be able to experience any of these emotions within the second list while experiencing any of those in the first. It's as if one's mind is incapable of feeling *angry* while feeling *elated*. Or *delighted* while being *lonely*.

5.3 Emotional change always follows a sequence

Within our unconscious minds we all have a type of syntax which controls what feelings we experience and when. This means that we may switch in an instant from one state to another. Perhaps you can remember a time when one minute you felt great and the next something seemed to happen inside you and the feeling changed to one of frustration, or sadness, or whatever else you may have felt?

If you were able to stop and analyse the circular sequence that your emotions flow through, you would be able to recognise that they always follow the same broad pattern. Perhaps you might feel elated, then self-conscious, then feel guilty for feeling so good, then seem to get stuck with guilt for quite a while.

Let us take an example which permits us to consider in more detail how we cross these emotional thresholds. Do you know of someone, or are you perhaps someone whom people say the following about. *"That guy, he just seems so cold at times, it's as if he doesn't realise how hurtful what he says is to me. He doesn't seem to do it on purpose, he just doesn't seem to notice what he's doing."*

In this scenario, this man has unconsciously created specific mechanisms within his mind which facilitate the following:

1. A belief structure about how to act with other people, in respect of treating them with empathy, based on previously real or imagined experiences within his own life.

2. A filtering mechanism which does not flag up any emotional responses from other people which are below a certain level.

This filtering mechanism can be seen when we consider how he would respond if challenged over his attitude. Probably he would not even realise that he was being cold, callous or suchlike, since these states are themselves beliefs about what those feelings are.

He may initially feel anger at having his approach challenged in this manner. Other people may attempt to play "the blame game" focusing attention on others and away from themselves.

5.4 How the sequence is created

Whenever a new belief is received it is incorporated into the existing structure by a process known as *Matching*. Take, for example, a child who is praised and feels proud. That feeling of *proud* may become matched to its nearest counterpart, for example, that of feeling *confident*. However, the actual structure will be determined by the level of emotional content which is contained within the memories.

This means that the belief structure will be organised around a framework of *primary beliefs* and *secondary beliefs*. The unconscious mind will achieve this since it will then be able to focus its energy on fulfilling the primary beliefs which, in turn, continue to ensure that the secondary beliefs (or lower order beliefs) are fulfilled.

6. How The Unconscious Mind Controls Our Behaviour

6.1 How we learn

Scientific discoveries have now enabled us to develop an understanding of the way in which many and varied automatic functions are carried out within our bodies. We now know that it is the unconscious mind which controls most of our automatic functions. This includes the deep, genetically-programmed drives, such as those for survival and procreation, and the simpler, learned, habitual patterns which are taught from an early age.

Most authorities acknowledge that our learning process can be defined as comprising four distinct steps, each of which uses the conscious and unconscious mind in different ways. Furthermore, if we recognise that we are all learning new ways of behaving and adding these to those which we already know, then it follows that we can be at one or more of these different stages at the same time, depending on what we are doing at that time.

1. *UNCONSCIOUS INCOMPETENCE*: This occurs when we don't know what we don't know. We can be anything from a child not knowing he doesn't know how to walk, because he has not tried it yet, to a person who has not realised that there is a better way of planning the day.

2. *CONSCIOUS INCOMPETENCE*: During this stage we now know what we don't know. Consider the same child's frustration now when he tries and fails to co-ordinate his limbs in order to stand on two legs and walk. Or that same person who can recognise that other people in the office are achieving more in less time and with less stress.

3. *CONSCIOUS COMPETENCE*: We have now identified and are learning the steps and processes to carry out the tasks that previously we found impossible. These tasks could range from walking or making toast through to driving a car or piloting an aircraft. During this learning phase, we have to filter everything through our conscious mind which means that we will process information at a slower pace than we would like. This could also include driving to a new place of work. This is a phase of frustration as we learn the right way from the wrong way. This will show up in the expression of concentration on the child's face as he attempts to consciously manipulate his muscles and to co-ordinate his body movements. The elation from success would also be noticed at this stage.

4. *UNCONSCIOUS COMPETENCE:* Once we have been able to master the specific processes, we can now consign the physical and emotional tasks to the unconscious mind. From this stage on, we will not notice ourselves carrying out the steps. Someone would state that he does what he does automatically and without thinking. This includes such examples as the young child who is now able to walk with fluidity and is quite nonchalant about the process. Or finding that taking the formerly-new journey to the office has become an automatic process and that we no longer notice certain signs or road junctions as we used to.

Once a learning has passed into the final stage we will no longer notice what is being thought or carried out, nor will we ever consciously stop to question how or why we are thinking as we are.

Clearly, the more quickly and easily a task, or a way of behaving, or a way of thinking, can be taken up to Level 4, *Unconscious Competence*, the more simplified someone will find his life. Provided, of course, that the methodology which he consigns to the deeper recesses of his unconscious mind is useful to him and has not been based on limiting incorrect beliefs.

It is the belief structures about how to act, think and do things which become consigned to our unconscious mind, which we, as therapists, deal with on a day-to-day basis. Naturally, we can, if necessary, create significant improvements in a client's learning process but we will usually find it necessary to assist the client in revising his beliefs about his attitudes first.

6.2 How the unconscious mind filters out information

The conscious mind is that part of our mind which is used to process the thinking of which we are aware. This includes such things as reading the words of this book, taking notice of the sounds outside the room, or actually carrying on a conversation. This part of our mind cannot do many things at once and various tests have indicated that the maximum number of discrete activities which can be administered by the conscious mind is seven, plus or minus two, depending on complexity.

The unconscious mind, however, has an amazingly large capacity to operate in a multi-tasking way since every other function within the human body is carried out, timed and monitored by the unconscious mind. This part of our mind can and does complete millions and millions of tasks per second. And of these, there are probably very few of which we are ever aware.

While sitting and reading this book, turning pages as you go, have you *consciously* caused or *consciously* noticed any of these things happening?

- the turning of the page

- adjustments in your seating position

- blinking

- understanding what each word in the text of the book meant to you

- the instantaneous connection of some of these meanings to your own experiences

- the ongoing process of ensuring that your breathing continues, that your heart beats and so on

All of these activities and functions will have been carried out by the direct or indirect action of different parts of your unconscious mind. In exactly the same way, your unconscious mind will have filtered all of your thoughts, memories and experiences so as to save you the trouble of having to go "back to basics" each time. Consider how much more difficult it would be for you if every time you were to read a word you had to look up its definition in a dictionary. No. Once you know what a word means, you accept its meaning as correct each time. This is similar to the way in which beliefs operate.

7. The Relationship Between Energy And Thought

7.1 A quantum viewpoint

Modern scientific research indicates that at the lowest level of form, that of the quantum, we don't exist. If we use this book as an example we can appreciate the mind-boggling effects of this statement. This book contains pages, pages are made of paper, paper contains molecules, molecules are comprised of atoms, atoms are bundles of energy when you approach the quantum level, and energy is 99.9999% absolute nothing, empty space.

It therefore follows that everything is made up of energy and also everything nearly totally doesn't exist.

Science has also provided us with further information on energy. Energy cannot be created or destroyed. It can only be changed, channelled or converted – in this context, through aligning and focusing a person's beliefs from multiple directions to a single direction. From this he will be able to achieve his desires from a position of ease, rather than fail from a position of tiredness and stress.

7.2 Mental energy

Most people are aware of how it is to feel physically exhausted but many do not believe that you can really be mentally exhausted. But by understanding how a belief structure operates and that the unconscious mind is burning up energy all the time to fulfil each and every belief, it is possible to become aware of how mental exhaustion occurs.

Energy is expended all the time, whether we are awake or asleep. A tremendous amount of energy can be expended when we are asleep, especially after significant changework has occurred, which then requires integration within the unconscious mind.

However, once we have assisted the client in realigning his beliefs so that all his beliefs for a single issue are congruent and focused in the same direction, he will find that he will use less energy to complete his tasks. Naturally, this energy now available may become used elsewhere and he is now presented with choice. He is no longer *"running around like a headless chicken"* (which was how one client expressed his previous lifestyle).

This change in the client's belief structure ensures that the appropriate behavioural change results and, in doing so, alleviates the client's confusion. This will usually show up the underlying beliefs which have been operating out of the client's conscious awareness and causing the problems in his life.

7.3 How a belief draws energy towards itself

Once a belief has been set in place, it will start to grow. The more emotionally powerful the originating incident was, the more energy the belief will have to start with. However, any and all beliefs will grow over time, be they positive or negative. This occurs through the client's unconscious processes which will draw into his life those events which each belief needs to stay continually fulfilled. As this happens, more and more energy becomes contained within the belief structure, as more and more thoughts become consolidated as one single structure.

If we consider for a moment the structure of a belief system, we find that it looks surprisingly similar to the format used to explain how atoms join together. The similarity is continued further when we recognise a further fact – the thoughts and beliefs closer to the centre have more emotional energy than those at the outer reaches. The significance of this fact is that your client is using an ever-increasing amount of energy all the time that he is fulfilling his beliefs.

This is similar to the property of mutual attraction possessed by all bodies that are made of matter. Science has revealed that the more dense an object is, the larger the gravitational force created – in turn drawing objects towards itself. Similarly, within a belief structure, two or more highly emotionally-charged primary beliefs at the centre of the structure will cause other thoughts and experiences to become attracted to them and these will in turn create secondary beliefs (or lower order beliefs).

This is self-perpetuating since the belief structure will be stronger and more able to draw towards itself thoughts and experiences from other structures, further increasing its own energy levels. This process can be analogised to the way in which a black hole, which is an extremely dense body, draws every type of energy towards itself, consuming more and more matter as it becomes heavier and heavier.

To explain how this would operate in a real situation, let us consider the example of someone who has a belief, formed in childhood, that he needs to be rejected. Until he identifies the originating cause and releases the pent up emotional energy, he will, unconsciously, always seek rejection. This will take a lot of time and energy to do. If, however, he were to find a partner who has a belief about never standing up for her rights, we have now an accident waiting to happen. The first person will be expending energy attempting to create situations whereby his partner will reject him, and his partner will be burning up energy in an attempt to keep them together. As time moves on these two people will generate more and more friction between them, both attempting to fulfil their ill-matched beliefs. Sooner or later something must give. This could be in the form of a therapeutic change, separation, illness or violence. One thing we can be sure of – the unreleased emotional energy will find a way out.

Within our lives, whatever we think is reflected in the experiences we have. This means that if we believe life to be hard, it will be. If we think life will be easy, it will be. Our unconscious mind will seek out situations which are in alignment with our beliefs, and where it cannot find those which agree with our beliefs, the ego will interpret the remainder in such a way that they will be seen to fit in some way.

As we move through time, this will mean that our mind will become filled with more and more experiences, all actually neutral but each interpreted in a certain way via our ego. This means that the more experiences we have, notice or are aware of, the more our beliefs are reinforced.

Let us use as an example a man who, as a child, was regularly told off by his parents for doing wrong. As a child, he is made to feel guilty. As he grows up, he continues to feel guilty. His mind will look at many of the different situations he experiences only in one way:

This means I am guilty.

But consider also that a part of him, as a boy, did not feel he was guilty. This is going to cause confusion since at some time he will feel guilty and, at other times, he will not. As time continues he will create more and more reference-experiences to justify why he feels guilty and also why he does not. By the time he comes to consult us, as a client, he is, no doubt, quite confused and also quite tired. This happens because his unconscious mind is trying to fulfil both opposing beliefs and, in doing so, is connecting more and more new experiences to the original beliefs in order to reinforce them.

However, if he were to rid himself of the belief that he is guilty and cease using up so much energy proving this to be true, then he would also not have to prove his innocence and further energy would be released. This concept of energy being released can be taken literally since within his mind an inordinate amount of energy will be being expended in an attempt to justify and to reinforce both of these opposing beliefs.

In this way beliefs can be compared to muscles. The more we use muscles, the more powerful they become. All muscles work in pairs or groups, providing opposing actions as required. If one muscle becomes detached or injured, the resulting lack of use causes it to wither and to become weaker.

This can be further recognised in the words we can apply to describe different states of being:

1   relaxed, balanced, calm, smooth, unwound, flexible, effective, efficient
2   obsessive, compulsive, intense, strict, possessed, dominated
3   detached, unfeeling, dispassionate, uncaring, indifferent, disinterested

The words within list 1 are what most people would consider to be healthy. Note that they do not indicate an absence of energy, more an absence of redirected or nervous energy. List 2 contains the words often applied to people who seem to be directing too much energy in one direction to the detriment of other areas of their lives. List 3 could be said to indicate those people who have switched off, those whose energy has been dissipated and is not available for use.

All these words can be considered to be beliefs (all have appeared in previous client lists). Therefore, it can be understood that each list would attract energy in a different way. People whose beliefs were more in line with list 1 would find their beliefs to be less draining, compared to those in lists 2 or 3.

7.4 The cyclic nature of beliefs

Building on the understanding of how beliefs are formed and how we project our internal experiences on to others, we must now ask ourselves how is it that sometimes we feel good and, at other times, we feel bad – both for no apparent reason. Most of us have probably had days when we have felt elated, unstoppable, finding ourselves just clicking with everybody we meet. Conversely, we can find ourselves feeling down, angry, easily hurt or depressed.

This can happen to everybody at different times and most people accept this changeability as a fact of life. However, it can be shown that in exactly the same way that the hands of a clock cannot express the time as 12.45 am and 2.28 pm at once, there are permutations of feelings which we cannot experience at the same time. Furthermore, we do not feel the same way consistently, we find ourselves flowing from one feeling state to another. This is natural and can be seen in many other naturally-occurring arenas of life. All phenomena in life can be in, at least, two states – we breathe in and out, pain comes and goes, hunger rises and – even if not fed – abates after a while. We can be laughing heartily and, the next minute, the same thing is no longer funny. Later, however, the same situation would be regarded as funny again.

What appears to happen is that the thoughts within our mind become connected in such a way that one emotional state flows naturally into another. The process which the mind uses to connect beliefs together is known as *matching*. The mind will interpret a thought in such a way as to generate a belief. Then the mind identifies what other beliefs are held which are similar or even totally opposite. These matching thoughts are then connected, permitting energy to flow from one to the other. This is how belief structures are formed.

This is a useful process if all the emotional states flow in a positive way but if we have had bad experiences then the opposite will occur. Consider a child whose parents went through a particularly messy and emotionally-charged divorce. Perhaps from this the child learned that relationships do not last and that relationships are false. This means that while the adult enjoys the building of relationships, he or she would begin to notice a certain falseness about his or her new partner and this would tend to let them both grow apart. This would confuse them immensely since at the start of a relationship everything was good and they would never guess that their own beliefs were causing the problem. They part and then off they would go to their next relationship, hoping for better luck next time.

It can be shown that the sequence of emotional change is always the same for a person, and that this syntax can be mapped out and then this circular change in emotions can be traced back to the originating cause. In this way we can begin to understand how we will actually switch from one type of feeling to another as we move through time.

7.5 How beliefs connect and conflict

All beliefs are controlled by the unconscious mind through the ego. This means that we are, therefore, never consciously aware of whether our beliefs are acting in a congruent fashion to support each other or, as is often the case, are in conflict with each other causing us distress and pain.

This can be revealed when a particular element of our life or of our client's life is reviewed with GOLD Counselling. During this process it is possible, firstly, to identify all the beliefs related to this element of life and then, secondly, to determine how they all fit together. It is only from this position that we can then be sure whether our beliefs are truly liberating instead of restricting.

Let us take an example of a man who wants to become more successful so that he can feel good about himself and better provide for his family. This he continually tries to do – unfortunately with only short-term success. He is, however, unaware of an unconscious belief that to be successful results in a failed marriage, since that is what happened to his parents. Until this belief is revised, he will continue his erratic successes and stay totally unaware of why this is happening.

Note that the way in which beliefs connect together is quite different from the rules of mathematics where one adds together all the positive numbers and all the negative numbers in order to generate an aggregate sum. The unconscious mind, via the ego, will fulfil each and every belief we hold. Therefore, at different times and, in different situations, each and every belief will be applied to interpret the world.

Consider the following example of beliefs or thoughts recorded by a client on the topic of *Relationships:*

A Gives happiness
B Unusual
C Not allowed

D Frightened

E Sad

The client who wrote those beliefs down found himself unconsciously drawn to experiencing each of those beliefs about the world for differing amounts of time throughout his life. This caused much confusion and consternation since he would not be aware of how he was actually causing his own problems on a day-to-day basis.

The difference between how beliefs cycle from one belief to another and how one would expect to combine a set of values mathematically must be clearly understood. To understand how this happens, let us assume that one could ask the client to allocate an arbitrary rating of either positive or negative to the intensity of emotions when experiencing the world through each belief.

F Gives happiness

G Unusual   +4

H Not allowed   +2

I Frightened   -3

J Sad   -6

                                                                                -5

By addition of the notional values, it would appear that the client would stay at an emotional level of -8, this being the sum of all the values. However, we know that all beliefs are cyclic, flowing from one state of belief to another. Therefore, the client will find himself moving from one belief to another in whatever order they are connected, experiencing highs and lows without any understanding of why. This lack of understanding can itself become a belief, one which will be fulfilled by the cyclical nature of the other beliefs held.

7.6 Lying is tiring

When we say the right thing to please others, even when we know it's not true, we suppress the release of emotional energy. Until released this will continue to stay within our body and will affect our day-to-day life in various ways.

When you are in a position whereby you must choose between what is and what should be, the mind will always choose to focus on what should be. This difference between reality and imagination will require further energy to keep the lie going, further draining your client's energy levels and possibly creating psychosomatic illnesses.

However, once your client is able to have an emotional release of the belief which is the lie, he will never need to hold on to that lie again. From then on, his energy levels will begin to rebuild and, as stated in Section 7.2, his new alignment will ensure he draws positive and not negative experiences into his life.

7.7 The self-organising system within the unconscious mind

It is, from this stage onwards, appropriate to consider and recognise that the unconscious mind processes beliefs as if they are each living structures, equivalent to a totally self-organising system. The unconscious mind controls and organises the overall structure and prioritises beliefs according to the type and strength of emotional content. This is because every thought, sensory input or memory once had a level of emotional input which is the prime element used by the unconscious mind to sort thoughts into beliefs.

Our research has meant that we have been able to design a process diagram which sets out exactly how the unconscious mind operates when it creates a belief structure. The flowchart opposite sets out the methodology which is used by the unconscious mind when doing this.

The unconscious mind is receiving new thoughts, ideas and sensory inputs all the time. Every one of these is either added to an existing belief structure, or is used with at least one other thought to create a new belief structure.

It can be seen that the unconscious mind applies a very simple but powerful sort program every time a new thought occurs. This means that it can efficiently and effectively sort and collate hundreds of thousands of thoughts. Under normal circumstances, we are only ever aware of a few thoughts – those with an emotional content above a certain level.

Flowchart to explain how a belief structure is created from individual thoughts

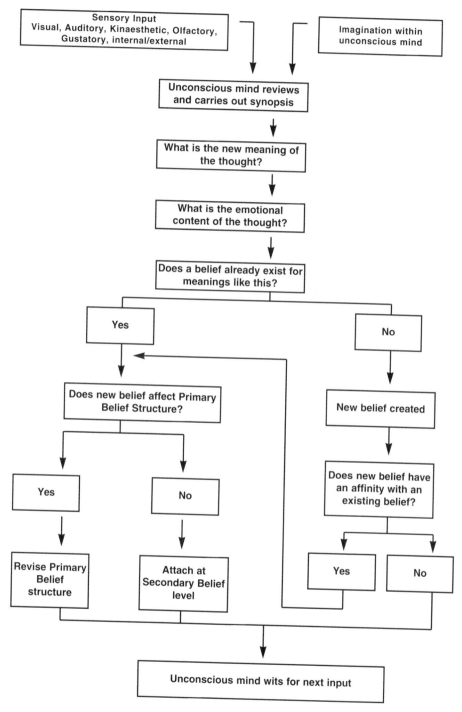

8. How Thoughts Are Remembered

8.1 What is a true memory?

How do you know that you know that you're right in what you remember? How do you know that you know that your memory hasn't failed you? When a national newspaper ran a series of television adverts in the mid 1980s, they showed just how easy it is for a group of people all watching the same incident to have different memories about it. Consider the scene. A frail old man is walking along the pavement. Suddenly, a dangerous-looking youth, shaven-headed and in jeans runs towards him and, just as the old man reaches the corner, the youth pushes him out of the way.

Next we cut to a different angle. In this we see a uniformed police officer running towards the youth. It seems that he is giving chase. And lastly, we are then presented with a wider-angled perspective. We see that both the youth and the policeman are both running towards the same old man. This is because the scaffolding above him has given way and in seconds he would be crushed beneath steel and rubble. Both were risking their lives to save his.

Only when you've been able to assimilate all the facts is it possible to determine the truth, but by whose definition is it the truth?

Facts are facts but interpretations are different. Consider how the legal system works. Both sides will aim to present cases which show their clients in the best light. Both are "true" and a jury is required to determine which truth is to be believed.

Where this is important for a therapist is that the memories which a client has are just that – memories. No-one can prove these memories are right or wrong. They are purely an interpretation of events. Our role is to ensure that the events can be interpreted, or sometimes reinterpreted, by our clients so as to release any limitations which the original view may have caused.

8.2 Emotional content

Most people are more able to remember things in which they have had an emotional involvement. It's as if emotion is the filter which is applied to determine whether the memory is stored with a lot of detail or with minimal detail. Consider two different meals in a restaurant. One you have with friends you value greatly, one with someone you find, frankly, quite boring. With the first event you will no doubt be able to recollect in greater detail and more easily the various facets of the event. Whereas in the second, its lack of emotional content renders the incident forgettable.

Another reason for thoughts or incidents to become stored is when the event was felt to be so important, so monumental to you that it actually altered your beliefs about the world. Consider how comfortable someone may feel walking along the same road on the way home from work for years, until on one particular day he is robbed at knife-point. This incident would be personal, emotionally very powerful, new and different, and force him to reconsider his beliefs in respect of personal safety. As a result this information would definitely become stored as a long-term memory, whether or not he can consciously remember the incident. Recognise that whether you consciously attempt to repress and deny the memory will not matter at all. Once the memory has been laid down within your mind it will influence you thereafter.

8.3 The effects of ageing

Most scientists involved in the research as to the way in which the human brain operates believe that we appear to utilise a small amount of the total volume available. Also, it is believed that if taught correctly, we can learn a phenomenal amount at an amazing rate. So why then is it that as people grow older, their capability to learn diminishes? It's certainly not because they've run out of space in their heads! Consider how some professors continue in their teaching posts for years, often long after their retirement, and their subjects are invariably cerebral, not physical.

The reason is due to the beliefs which have already been formed within that person at an earlier time. To use an analogy to explain, let us consider the petrol gauge in a car. This operates by picking up information in the petrol tank as to the level of capacity in the tank. Too much and one could run out of fuel. Too little capacity and you've got a full tank. But what would happen if the wrong sender was fitted? Say a sender for an eight-gallon tank on a ten-gallon car? The gauge on the dashboard would always understate the capacity left over. Obviously, when filling up at a petrol station this error may be noticed, but all the time one is reading the instruments in the car, the error would be compounded.

And this is what happens with people as they age. It is usual to learn at school. Afterwards, most people will seek employment and then spend the majority of their years working not learning. Because this is the accepted way of thinking and behaving, this is what happens. If you were to review the beliefs of older, retired people about learning, you would identify significant limiters as to being too old, not my place, letting the youngsters have a go, and so on. In doing so they are fulfilling their beliefs, which are that as they've become older they could not learn any more. Many times older people use the phrase "You can't teach an old dog new tricks" as an attempt to justify the reason why they don't want to change. As therapists we must recognise this for what it really is. They are saying "can't" when they really mean "won't". This is a belief and this would need to be questioned and revised before change will occur.

A further example of how age and beliefs are inter-related can be revealed when considering the effects of retirement on the male population. Some men look forward to retirement since to them it means that they can do new things with their new-found time. Whereas others not long after retirement find themselves succumbing to illness, boredom and listlessness. It's as if, to them, to retire from work is to retire from life.

8.4 Every thought influences

Every single event which we have experienced, either by our external senses, such as sight or touch, or our internal senses, including anything we have imagined or dreamt, will have influenced us in some way. Some events may have become less important as we have grown up or changed our social situations but at different times in our lives every thought must have at some time influenced us.

To elaborate further on this, consider not only how effective but also how subtle some advertising is. Most adverts don't sell purely the object for which you will be handing over your hard-earned money. No. They sell you the image, how you imagine you will look/feel/behave/be treated by others because you have wisely chosen their product. In a single day of travelling through an average town we are bombarded by hundreds, if not thousands, of different adverts. Each one will generate thoughts in our mind, either positive, negative or neutral. All of these thoughts come together to form a picture of what you like or dislike and so on and once you have purchased the product – you in turn become an advert. This means that the personality which you develop may be influenced in ways by sources which you didn't even realise were there.

8.5 Memory is not accurate

Lying takes so much time and takes up so much energy. Most people just don't remember everything and when you read about the mental feats of people who memorise lists of numbers you can realise that specific techniques are required. It, therefore, follows that most people will not record everything with clarity. Often we quite honestly can't remember something. So we have to skirt around it, remembering bits at a time, until the whole memory is reformed once again. However, if a story were fabricated all that would exist in someone's mind would be the framework he had built.

Often, when remembering a memory we notice that something about the same memory is now different. This flexibility in recall is a natural phenomenon and through applying relaxation techniques to remove further blockages to recall, even more detail can be ascertained.

8.6 Types of memory

Research shows that we all appear to have different types of memory and that one or more types are used whenever we consign an event to our unconscious mind. Understanding which type is being presented by your client will ensure that you can achieve clarity when he is, consciously or not, putting up barriers to recall.

1. **EVENT MEMORY** is the ability to recall an incident at a particular time, in a particular place.

2. **ROTE MEMORY** occurs when something has been carried out so many times that differences between each occasion have been lost. This is more vague than event memory and can apply when one of the events was distressing.

3. **PERIOD MEMORY** occurs when someone only seems to have a feeling about a large amount of time, perhaps feeling that all school was boring or lonely. This has obviously a large number of individual

memories bundled together and can be influenced by a desire not to delve too deeply into the past.

4. **SCENIC MEMORY** occurs when someone has a memory of a place, such as a house he has lived in, but only experiences it visually. To expand this we would need to encourage him to access information from his mind about what he might be seeing, hearing or feeling.

5. **SCREEN MEMORY** happens when we think we know why we feel or act the way we do, whereas this is really a displacement, a substitution for the real reason. This may occur due to the negative effects of positive thinking, (see Chapter 11) or due to ongoing symptom-substitution, or denial.

6. **FUZZY MEMORY** effects occur when the unconscious mind fills in missing parts of information with that which it believes to be true, even though there is no justification for its actions.

It is not always realised how powerful the unconscious mind's desire to simplify its actions really is. This is embodied within the concept of Fuzzy Memory. You can carry out a simple experiment to experience first-hand how Fuzzy Memory affects all of us.

Take a piece of white A4 paper and mark on it two black circles. Now choose either one and make a hole through it. Next, hold the paper by either of the bottom corners and close one eye. Slowly bring the sheet of paper towards your face while focusing your open eye on the unpierced black circle. Keep aware of the hole using peripheral vision and notice what happens as you bring the sheet closer. At a certain distance the hole will "disappear". In fact, your unconscious mind has assumed that this area is as solid, as is the rest of the paper, and fills in the missing information for you. However, it is wrong. This is what the unconscious mind will do with memories causing you to believe certain things when, in fact, they are fabrications from your own unconscious mind.

8.7 Tricks of the eye – the desire for simplicity

Once we believe something to be true, we will unconsciously look for ways to prove it so. Furthermore, we will often see and experience things, not as they are but as we expect them to be. Many automatic patterns are built up in this way.

We are sure that most of you reading this book will have seen examples of those pictures which are designed to trick the eye. One minute the image is of a candlestick and the next you can see two faces looking at each other. Or perhaps you have seen some of the graphics created by the artist M.C. Escher. He used the two dimensions of paper to distort the reader's viewpoint and create apparently impossible situations such as water running uphill, never-ending staircases, or rooms without separate inside walls or outside walls.

Many people use this technique outside their driveways when they put up a notice, in blue which says "POLITE NOTICE – NO PARKING". The mind expects to see POLICE and, therefore, that is what we believe we see.

9. *Language, Words And Speech*

9.1 The need for communication

It is fascinating to consider that every civilisation which has ever inhabited our planet at whatever time in its history has felt the need to develop ways of recording the things which it has felt, heard or seen. From such diverse places as cave paintings, stone tablets, papyrus rolls and village chants, we have always sought a medium to express how those things that we have experienced have affected us.

Some of these mediums of expression have been focused on the supposed true facts, such as written texts, historical paintings and photographs. Other methods have been developed to enable feelings or abstract interpretations of the writers or artists or designers to be expressed with the hope that they would be understood by others in the same way.

It is this attempt to enable others to understand the meaning within the communication which has been a challenge ever since the earliest days of developing methods of communication. While there has not, as yet, been developed a means of knowing exactly what someone else is feeling, seeing or hearing, by using language in an artful way it is possible to determine what the experience has meant to him.

It therefore follows that dependent on both the level of competence held by the user and the skills available to him, it is possible to clarify the meaning of the experience to a greater or lesser degree.

9.2 Misunderstandings and misinterpretations

Have you ever been in, or can you imagine, a situation whereby in talking to someone you have to correct his interpretation of your words? *"No. That's not what I mean. What I meant was..."* Or perhaps you have thought you understood someone completely and then realised that his interpretation of events had been distinctly different to yours. Everyone that you ever come into contact with will have had different experiences and will have grown up in different ways. Accordingly, there will be a difference between what you say and how it is understood. Furthermore, words have different meanings to all of us. We use words in an attempt to say what we mean. We will always use our best endeavours to select words which best express the message we want to get across.

Perhaps as children or even as adults you have played games that are designed to connect your skills of word association. This includes such things as "Chinese Whispers" and games in which, by changing contexts, different meanings for words have to be found.

This is one of the reasons why learning a language can become so difficult for some people, because when interacting with others there exists many possibilities for misinterpretations and subsequent justifications.

> "Mortals are wrapped in words the way a spider wraps flies in gossamer. In this case you are both spider and fly because you imprison yourself in your own web."
>
> Deepak Chopra
> *The Way Of The Wizard*

9.3 The difference between language and words

Within the unconscious mind, a word does not have just a meaning, it has a connection to other words in a linguistic daisy-chain – just as one memory will lead to another and another and so on. If we are able to follow these chains, we are then able to understand the deeper significance which has been attached by the client's unconscious mind to the words which he is using.

This example from an actual session will explain further. A client, who had repressed his emotions, recollects reading Star Trek annuals as a child and imagining himself as Mr Spock. After releasing this memory he later found himself connecting two further incidents which were related to the first by language.

As a teenager, his favourite aircraft was the *Avro Vulcan* and his favourite television series was *The Prisoner*. The client originally believed that he "just liked" the *Vulcan*. Although he made many aircraft models he never once felt the need to build a model of the *Vulcan*. This was his unconscious mind's way of using words to indicate the underlying symptom. In the series *The Prisoner*, the main character was captured and held against his will. The character was very cold and logical, similar to Mr Spock, and for years the client had been interested in purchasing a *Lotus Super 7* – the car used by the character. On further reflection, the client realised that he had heard that the character in *The Prisoner* had used the *Lotus* before the client had even seen the series. It was only years later that he actually sat down and watched the series.

Once the underlying cause had been released, along with his need for certain words to be in his mind, his interest in the aircraft and the television series shifted to one of neutrality. This indicated that his attraction to these things was the product of the original way of thinking about feelings and not from other more naturally-explained causes.

This example also reveals that the chronological effect of thoughts within the mind should be measured by reference to the client and not to any external and arbitrary clocks.

This leads us to the pre-supposition that a specific word is that specific word because it is not another – it is different from any other word. A word will have a value because of its difference from others. Furthermore, once something becomes labelled within our minds, we always refer to that label when we are really referring to the object.

9.4 The problem with confusing language and speech

It is important to recognise that there exists significant differences between language and speech and that these differences are of supreme importance when treating clients.

Language is a set of non-verbal symbols used to represent thoughts and feelings. Speech is vocal communication. Another interpretation is that speech is what we use to communicate to others, language is what we use ourselves. There needs to be two or more people for there to be any speech, whereas we can understand language internally.

As soon as someone starts speaking he is unconsciously giving an identity to the person to whom he is talking. Consider also what happens in an alternative scenario whereby someone's identity is taken away from him. A girl is "sent to Coventry" by her classmates because of something she believes she has done wrong. This act of not talking to her removes her from the inter-action of the class and ignores her existence.

As soon as you speak you are, at an unconscious level, selecting from all your thoughts and interpretations of language AND also unconsciously considering the other person as to what to say to him. When a client speaks, therefore, the words he uses have a significance in excess of that which is at first apparent.

This can be captured in the following phrase :

The words I use mean more than I mean in using them.

All speech carries meanings which are below the conscious awareness of the person speaking. Within therapeutic situations, this means that by being able to identify the links in the client's language, and making the appropriate connections, we can facilitate change.

9.5 The link between symptoms and language

Within the unconscious mind, language is used to store our thoughts. In this way, symptoms will be found to relate and link to specific words used by the client.

Although we know that at birth a baby cannot understand language, we know that he can hear language. Consider for a moment if you were on a train and heard two people conversing in a foreign language. While you may not be able to understand what is being said you could hear what is being said. In effect, the language that the baby will come to use exists before the baby does. As a child grows up and can understand language, he will learn to do the things which the words mean.

If we use another example from the work carried out with another client you should then be able to understand how this would come to light in practice. A client had been troubled by problems with money for many years. From the work carried out he seemed always to be waiting and hoping that his family would help him out when he got into financial difficulties. A particular phrase he often used (but didn't notice the significance of himself) was of being "bailed out".

Once he had finally reached financial rock-bottom, he did in fact ask his family for help. The result was exactly what he had hoped would not happen. They refused. They would not help him, realising this was, for him, initially, a very painful and traumatic experience. However, he was then able to understand that for years he had been waiting, to use his own words, "for my ship to come in." As a postscript, he later advised us that while watching television one day when visiting his family, he saw a programme which, in turn, jogged his memory to a series which he used to watch as a child. Its name was *When The Boat Comes In* and was, in his own words, "set in a poor fishing village where no-one had anything of financial value".

Needless to say, the usage of the phrase "bail me out" has stopped.

If we take the concept of symptoms being inextricably linked to words, we can realise their obvious effects in such things as hypochondria. In this, a patient will be convinced that a specific part of his body has a particular problem, even though all medical interventions have denied this fact. By determining the underlying meaning of the words the client is using to denote the area of his body with the problem, the link to the underlying unconscious symptom will be revealed. Once this is brought to the surface of consciousness the symptom will disappear since it is no longer needed.

In this way, the therapist needs to listen for and notice the correlation between the presenting symptoms and the actions which the client takes. The client's unconscious mind will indicate the actual cause of the problem through language and, therefore, we could equate the symptoms with words trapped in his body trying to get out by any means possible.

Section Two:

What Is GOLD Counselling?

Introduction to Section Two

Having read Section One you should now understand how the mind works at a technical level. Within Section Two you will find documented the procedures to use through which it is possible to create a radical shift in a person's beliefs and enable him to instantly and permanently change his beliefs into something empowering instead of restricting.

10. Specific Pre-Suppositions Within GOLD Counselling

10.1 Overview

Just as with NLP, Transactional Analysis, Gestalt Therapy and Inner-Child Counselling and many other therapeutic approaches, within the framework of the GOLD Counselling techniques there are specific pre-suppositions which need to be understood in order to ensure your success with its application.

When you first review these pre-suppositions, some of you may feel that they can't be right, that they seem illogical, impossible even. Well, we have found them **all** to be correct. As you continue to develop your understanding of this method, your realisation will expand to appreciate that each pre-supposition fits exquisitely within each instance of the GOLD Counselling techniques applied. We have found these pre-suppositions to be accurate every time and they form the foundations, the building blocks from which the specific techniques have been developed.

By keeping these pre-suppositions close to your awareness while working with your clients, you will understand with much more clarity why it is that certain things may be happening in their lives right now.

The pre-suppositions have been found to divide into two groups: Structural and Functional.

10.2 Structural pre-suppositions

Structural pre-suppositions can be used to identify the way in which the mind combines and collates individual thoughts which are then turned into actual living beliefs. Once these pre-suppositions are understood, you will realise how the unconscious mind will keep together all the various beliefs and ensure that all are fulfilled, at whatever cost.

1. The map *is* the territory. The way in which a person experiences the world is absolutely correct, based on all his experiences from whatever sources. In factual terms it may not be accurate, but it is the way in which he experiences the world and, therefore, that *is* how it is for him.

2. Opposing beliefs *do not* imply a contradiction. The unconscious mind will in one instant fulfil positive, life-enhancing beliefs and then, in a second, change and begin to fulfil negative, even harmful, beliefs without question.

3. There is no pre-set structure or pre-set framework that beliefs form. The brain is a self-organising system and, accordingly, there is no structure – the structure is the structure.

4. The mind is minimalistic. It will fulfil *any and all* beliefs using the simplest and most direct way possible.

5. To achieve a goal or feeling or objective, one must first remove the beliefs that are being fulfilled which are exactly 180° in the opposite direction. Rather than add positive thinking, *remove* negative thinking.

6. Every belief cycle will contain two or more beliefs, all of which are structured according to its level of *emotional* content.

7. A belief cell contains the interpretation of the event which includes the physical and emotional effect as well as the visual image.

10.3 Functional pre-suppositions

An understanding of functional pre-suppositions will enable the therapist to realise how the mind will continue to fulfil past, present and future beliefs, good, bad or indifferent, until acted on by the GOLD Counselling technique.

1. The unconscious mind does not understand past tense. Any beliefs installed in the past are still believed in the present. It only understands what *"is"*, never what *"was"*.

2. The unconscious mind cannot carry out instructions to achieve a state of being in the future tense. Any states or outcomes desired in the future must have already been achieved in the present. It only understands what *"is"*, never *"to be"*.

3. The unconscious mind does not think, it just *does*. Automatically and repeatedly until told to do otherwise.

4. We never get what we want unless what we want is what we are. We are what we think and, therefore, we are our thoughts.

5. We live our lives by every belief we have. We are now the sum total of all that we have ever believed.

6. The unconscious mind will fulfil all beliefs within the unconscious mind at all times.

7. *All* thought is creative.

8. In the unconscious mind it is not the event, but rather the *interpretation* of the event, which is stored.

9. The symptom is the solution. That is to say the symptoms displayed by the client is the solution that the mind has found to deal with an event. The solution/symptom is based upon the information and resources available to the client at the time of the event.

11. Problems With Instilling Positive Thinking

As you reflect on the pre-suppositions listed in Chapter 9, it is possible now to understand why various other methods, which you may have used to help either yourself or your clients, will have been doomed to failure as time progressed. Perhaps this will also clarify why certain apparent "successes" have turned into "failures" over time.

This would be because no attempt was made to remove the harmful, limiting beliefs which were actually causing the problem. All that occurred was that good, positive beliefs were placed over these. When you under-stand this, it is possible to realise the folly of so many so-called self-improvement techniques.

However, if it were possible to totally and permanently remove the limiting belief, all that would remain within the person's unconscious mind would be the positive belief, and this would move the person forward to the person which he wishes to become.

Unfortunately, most of us are unable to identify what it is that is actually limiting us. This is often because the area of our life in which we must look may contain some unpleasant memories; so we elect to cover these up with a dose of positive thinking and get on with trying to do the best we can. To separate these so-called techniques from GOLD Counselling we have named these approaches *"Fool's Gold"*.

To understand further the problems associated with this approach, imagine what would happen in the following situation. A man buys an old house to live in and to slowly renovate. Initially filled with enthusiasm, he sets himself a schedule to rebuild all the rooms and to carry out whatever is needed to rectify any problems. However, as time moves on, he keeps on finding himself making excuses not to start work in two of the rooms. *"They're not too bad"*, he says. *"Perhaps I'll wait a bit longer"* he thinks. He seems to ignore the fact that these two rooms are both in need of major structural work, and that these are the rooms which contain the strength-ening supports for the whole house.

If someone uses these techniques, his approach is like having first bought an old property and then to paper over the cracks in the walls so that they can't be seen. Or instead of removing the roots of weeds in the garden, cutting them down to the surface so that they don't show followed by planting new shrubs in the same ground and hoping that all will be well.

Many of the people with whom we have worked using this technique had already tried many other positive-thinking-based techniques, albeit unsuccessfully. Once they understood how GOLD Counselling works they then either dropped the old techniques totally, or incorporated their new learnings into their existing methodologies.

The types of techniques which have within them all the limitations previously mentioned would include such approaches as:

- positive thinking
- affirmations
- progressive de-sensitisation
- goal-setting
- writing out positive versions of negative beliefs
- visualisation
- reading motivational literature
- suggestion therapy
- wishing or hoping
- New Year's resolutions
- denial, or pretending that those things did not really happen

While all of these approaches can generate partial and short-term successes, no attempt is made to remove the negative belief which is underpinning the existing negative belief structure. Taking the analogy of the old house, eventually the cracks will get worse, connecting to cracks in other parts of the walls. Left unattended, the house itself could become worse and worse, perhaps weakening those nearby.

Exponents of these techniques believe and act as if by taking ten or twenty positive beliefs and using them to smother a few negative beliefs, all will be well.

This approach fails, and it fails because, in itself, it fails to incorporate the learning embodied in GOLD Counselling pre-supposition 10.2.2. Opposing beliefs *do not* imply a contradiction. The unconscious mind will in one instant fulfil positive, life-enhancing beliefs and then, in a second, change and begin to fulfil negative, even harmful, beliefs without question.

Furthermore, in just the same way as when growing a seed from a plant, the seed requires regular tending and nurturing, so do new beliefs. Those already in existence have more power over the newcomers and will further reinforce their influence, sucking energy away from the new ways of thinking.

If, however, someone does appear to derive a benefit from any of the foregoing techniques, then he will have unknowingly caused the symptom to substitute itself into another facet of his life. Take, for example, someone who has a lack of confidence. If he were to recite affirmations which are constructed to tell himself that he is now a confident person, he may well become confident. But over the coming days he may begin to notice a fresh problem rearing its head. Until the originating cause is removed, symptom substitution will continue.

A further danger in using any of these techniques is that by the time a client presents himself for treatment, the symptom that he may consider to be the problem may be as a result of many shifts and displacements from the originating cause. In this way, positive thinking actually worsens the situation, rather than improves it.

This was eloquently expressed by Carl Gustav Jung (1969) who wrote:

> *"A neurosis is truly removed only when it has removed the false attitude of the ego. We do not cure it, it cures us. A man is ill, but the illness is nature's attempt to heal him, and what the neurotic throws away as absolutely worthless contains the **true gold** we should never have found elsewhere."*

12. The GOLD Counselling Language Patterns

12.1 Overview

As explained within Chapter 9, the language used by a client when explaining his problem will provide us with an enormous amount of information about his symptoms and the underlying causes. Therefore by understanding what the language used by your client actually means, not only to him as he understands it but also at a deeper unconscious level, we can identify where change needs to occur.

12.2 Language patterns

If you have an appreciation of the importance that language holds within NLP, you will no doubt expect that within GOLD Counselling a specific language pattern has been developed to ensure the success of the technique. The precise language which is used is important since inappropriate guidance by the therapist would affect the direction along which the analysis progresses.

For example, if a particular belief such as *"I'm no good"* exists, the therapist needs to determine where that came from by allowing the client to re-experience the originating event, and not just to discuss the incident in a logical manner. The client will have logically analysed his memories, perhaps for years to no avail. What he now requires is an alternative way of understanding the situation.

If we consider the language systems as developed within NLP, we find that two models have been created, each with specific uses and each dovetailing into the other, combining perfectly to fulfil the language patterns of NLP.

The first set of language patterns was developed during the early 1970s and was derived from the ongoing study of certain therapists who were regularly using certain questions and language structures while working with their clients. This language pattern contained within it a level of precision, not normally found in everyday conversational language, and became known as the **Precision Model**, or the **Meta-model** (Bandler & Grinder, 1975). Its use enables you to drill down into the information being given to you by a client so that you can begin to question the specific issues that are underlying the deep structure of the actual problem he has.

The second language pattern that was developed became known as the **Milton model**, named after Milton Erickson, and was in effect the exact opposite of the Precision Model. Its structure was developed in a way that meant the language would bypass the analytical part of the mind and be accepted by the unconscious mind without any interference or conscious intervention.

12.3 GOLD Counselling language patterns

The language used within GOLD Counselling has in itself been developed to enable the detailed analysis of individual beliefs to be carried out in a simple and accurate manner. In the same way that the Meta-model is very precise and the Milton model is very vague, the GOLD Counselling language has been developed to be specifically vague.

Consider the different effects of the following questions on the client's problem.

Client: *I don't seem to be able to give up smoking.*

Meta-model questions:

Therapist: *How do you know that you don't seem able to?*

What else don't you seem able to do?

What would happen if you did give up smoking?

Milton model questions:

Therapist: *So, are there many things that you've not been able to give up?*

It may be that you just don't give up for long enough?

What's important for you in giving up smoking?

GOLD Counselling questions:

Therapist: *Where did I learn to believe the belief that I don't seem able to give up smoking?*

What happened to me to lead me to believe the belief that I don't seem able to give up smoking?

How did I learn to believe the belief that I don't seem able to give up smoking?

The Meta-model and the Milton model will cause the client to look at his problem from a different perspective, but only GOLD Counselling questioning will direct the client back to the originating time when the belief was first installed.

An understanding of both the Meta-model and the Milton model will significantly enhance your capabilities to work with GOLD Counselling. This is because when working with the GOLD method you are presented on paper with the actual language which expresses the unconscious thoughts which your client believes all the time – his thoughts are fulfilling his beliefs. Each one in turn is being fulfilled – some for just an instant, some for longer periods of time. This cyclic nature is related to the amount of energy that the client is expending in fulfilling his beliefs. Further information about how energy is used with beliefs will be found in Chapter 7.

Let us take this as an example. Suppose that in a GOLD Counselling analysis to identify where someone first developed an inability to ask questions in public, one of the central thoughts was as follows:

"I'd always get told off, now."

This sentence reveals, not just a grammatical error, but in addition a deeply-held unconscious belief that he is still being told off, and this is linked to the current problem. Readers may notice that this is similar to the errors perpetrated by the unconscious mind which were documented by Sigmund Freud and later given the unofficial name "Freudian slips." This type of language was also developed and codified from the modelling of Milton Erickson and forms part of the ambiguity patterns, such as syntactic ambiguity and phonetic ambiguity. This closeness of language indicates that all patterns are being derived from the same sources deep within the unconscious mind.

13. How To Create A GOLD Counselling Topic List

13.1 Subject selection

In order to understand which thoughts your client holds as primary beliefs, he must first create a list detailing all his thoughts about the chosen topic. This topic list should contain ALL of the beliefs, memories, and comments that come into his conscious mind when he considers the chosen topic. Some may be positive and others negative. Some may be clearly related and others, apparently unconnected.

It is essential that your client write down EVERY thought that comes into his mind. He must NOT consciously delete any. Furthermore, he must be instructed to write down all that he believes either all the time or sometimes and NOT what he wants to believe, or tries to believe. The latter types of beliefs are found within affirmations and positive thinking and its problematic influence will be elaborated on further in Chapter 16. Suffice it to say that we consider this type of thinking to be "Fool's Gold" since what it apparently offers is, in effect, worthless.

> "There is nothing worse than self-deception when the deceiver is always within us."
>
> Plato

The thoughts that enter your client's conscious mind will be many and varied. Some will be words and others will be sentences. There may be feelings, sounds, sentences or whole paragraphs. In some cases the thoughts will be very symbolic, almost dream-like. Each and every one MUST be written down.

The topic for which a list is constructed will be based on a specific topic, such as Happiness, Wealth, Stress or Pain. The topic may have been selected either by the client although based on your understanding of the presenting symptoms or you will have selected a topic yourself.

From the information presented in the topic list we are then able to determine how the experiences of the client have led to the formation of specific beliefs. It is from these beliefs that his choices about how to carry on his life have been formed.

To enable you to understand the different types of subjects, which could be used as a topic, we have listed below a few examples:

Example Topic Headings

Group A			Group B
I am/me	Relationships	Love	Fear
Expressing myself	Commitment	Playing	Illness
Accepting	Friends	Happiness	Cancer
Living	Feelings	Work	Death/Dying
Change	Partners	Driving	Pain
Money	Parents	Studying/Learning	Stress
Success	Sexuality	Exercise	Dyslexia

Our experience with GOLD Counselling has revealed that it is a powerful analytical technique. We would recommend that all prospective users start by working with the headings shown above in group A. It is only once you have fully understood how the GOLD technique operates and have successfully worked through all the above topics that we would suggest you develop a GOLD Counselling analysis on other topics such as those in group B.

13.2 Selecting the topic on which to work

It is probable that when a client comes to you he will already have formed an opinion about what his problem is and what is probably either causing it now or first caused it in the past. As therapists, however, we need to recognise that the mechanism he is using in an attempt to identify the area to be corrected is, in itself, part of the problem. We must, therefore, assume that he does not know what the true underlying reason behind his current situation is. This also applies to any unstructured self-analysis. Your ego's prime reason for existence is to fulfil all the beliefs you hold. Therefore, it will do whatever it needs to do in order to distract you from the real cause, since this would mean that the ego would have to undergo change.

We must, therefore, select an element of the client's life experiences which is general enough to encompass the broad scope of the problem as he sees it while still being open-ended enough to permit the unconscious mind to let the true reason come through. This is achieved by selecting a topic heading. This topic will be used to focus the client's unconscious mind and will ensure that all the relevant beliefs are revealed.

As an example, consider a client who comes along for help and expresses the problem as:

Well, it's all to do with my childhood, you know. My father used to beat me and bully me all the time.

If we were to select the topic as:

The effects of my father's bullying

we would achieve limited success. However, by suggesting topic headings such as Bullying, My Father or My Parents a much more wide-ranging selection of beliefs would be generated. From these we would then be able to locate the actual beliefs which are still in force now and causing the apparently-unwanted situation to continue.

The unconscious mind has a very precise way of using words. Each word which is held has a specific meaning related directly to the thought from which it first came. Therefore, one must apply a similar precision when specifying a topic on which to work. A balance needs to be achieved between selecting a topic which is too widely defined, since information which is important but irrelevant to the particular issue will be revealed, against selecting a topic which is so precise that the originating cause is inadvertently pre-supposed. This pre-supposition is what the client's mind has already done for him but it has not effected a cure.

A brief example of possible topic headings has been listed below:

I am
Me
Life for me is…
Work
Love
Relationships
Parenting
Money
Success
Failure
Exams
Happiness
Feelings

It can be seen that while these topic headings are very concise, the areas of one's life which they cover are wide. This permits the unconscious mind to interpret the topic in whatever way it needs to, ensuring that the long-held thoughts on the topic can be revealed.

It is often found that where two topics are worked on together, similar thoughts are found on both lists. This is expected and natural. Within the ego all our beliefs are linked together – therefore our thoughts in one area of our life, perhaps relationships, will permeate into our thoughts on something else, perhaps happiness. The positive effect of this is that in changing one part of our ego, additional unexpected and beneficial change will be felt in other areas of our life.

This is why whenever one is working with a client on a single and specific topic area, we would recommend asking the client to generate a list of beliefs on the topic of *I am.* This will reveal significant beliefs about the client and can be used to identify where further repair-work may be required.

It can often be useful to work with a client by asking him to prepare two beliefs lists, each opposite to the other. If a client feels that he has a problem with not succeeding enough in life, ask him to prepare a belief list on both *Success* and *Failure.* Listen to his language. Although he may suggest the problem is in one sphere of his life, other indications may reveal that this is not so. Recognise that his unconscious mind will probably be signalling the area for work, although the client will not be able to notice this, since his ego will be protecting him from this information.

13.3 Writing the GOLD Counselling topic list

It is essential that your client is able to access the appropriate state while constructing his list. To do this you may need to show him how best to relax and focus his mind, perhaps with the use of simple relaxation techniques such as control of breathing. Alternatively for those of you with NLP knowledge, finger anchoring, New Behaviour Generator or a Circle of Excellence could be found to be useful to install in him the appropriate resources of previous memories when he experienced comfort or calmness thus creating the required state.

Once you have been able to allow him to access the required state, you should instruct him as follows:

1. to sit calmly and quietly in a place that is right for him in which it is unlikely that he will be disturbed

2. to write the chosen topic on the head of a piece of paper with only the topic as a header

3. to focus on the topic and as he focuses on the topic, to write in sequence down the paper, each and every thought that comes into his mind

4. to write whatever thoughts enter the mind, letting his unconscious mind dictate the path along which the thoughts move

5. to write down whatever the thought is

6. to allow no justification – whatever comes to mind is OK and should be noted down

7. to write down items even if they are not understood or are irrational or unexpected, without judgment

8. to write down items even if they appear to conflict with or contradict other items on the list

9. to ignore any apparent errors of grammar, punctuation or mixtures of past, present or future tense

10. to compile a list of between ten and thirty items on the chosen topic

When preparing the list, each item should have a letter allocated in the left margin, starting with capital A. If the list exceeds twenty-six items, continue with AA, AB, AC and so on. Letters and not numbers should be used.

Analysis has shown that the ideal length for a list is from ten to thirty items. By suggesting to your client that he keeps his list short, this acts as a suggestion to his unconscious mind. The unconscious mind then presents the relevant information within a list of the appropriate size.

Once this list is prepared and a belief map has been created, you will often be presented with information which indicates where other work will be required to assist your client. This is because thoughts are not independent;

all are inter-related. Therefore, in presenting information on a single topic, this topic may actually be related to another issue. This can be compared to a family tree, where all the individual levels and families are connected by ones before them back to the first family members.

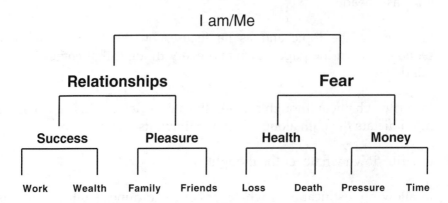

In order to enable you to begin to understand what a GOLD Counselling list would resemble when completed by a client, we have included an example of an actual list produced by a client on the topic of **"Relationships"**. This was produced following exactly the same instructions as those included in this chapter.

Topic: *Relationships*

A   Grumpy

B   Hard

C   Take time

D   Good sometimes

E   Rough

F   Crafty

G   Enjoyable

H   Never last

I   Always problems

J   Hidden agendas

K   Love

L   Not much love

M   Difficult

13.4 Linking the items on the list

On completing the previous steps, you will now be presented with a list, generated with the full assistance of your client's unconscious mind, which gives details of the main beliefs about the chosen topic. The linking of the list will reveal both the **primary** and **secondary beliefs** in the client's belief system. The primary beliefs are in effect the foundations and the secondary beliefs the building blocks. It might have been possible for your client to have continued the list further; some lists have comprised over one hundred items. However, by suggesting to the unconscious mind the desired length of the list, those items deemed most important will have surfaced.

The next step in the procedure is to ask your client to scan through each of the items on his list and, as if without any conscious thought, to connect all of these together. Instruct your client to look at the first item on the list and associate it to any other item on the list by writing the letter of the selected item alongside the first item. Then look at the second item and once more select an item from the list and write that letter alongside the second item. Continue until all the items on the list have been selected.

When doing this, there are specific instructions, which he should be given:

1. to let his unconscious mind do the process naturally

2. to recognise that no letter can link back to itself

3. to ensure that one item can connect to only one other item

4. to note that several items can all link to the same item

5. to emphasise that whatever way he feels he should connect the list is correct – there is no right or wrong way to connect each item

6. to ensure that there are no duplicated or similar words on the list

If, after completing the list, a word or phrase is found to have been duplicated, this should be challenged and your client should be instructed either to delete it or to replace it with a fresh item.

The example below shows how the belief list for the topic "Relationships" appeared once it was completed with each item on it linked correctly.

Pay particular attention to the letters **I, M and F** (*primary beliefs*) in one group and **H and K** (*primary beliefs*) in the other, as these form the basis of the client's belief system. The circular loop that these letters form when linked are in effect the client's circular reality.

All the remaining attached letters are secondary beliefs that only exist while supported by a primary belief. The secondary beliefs can only be experienced while supported by a primary belief. Once the primary belief has been removed or altered the secondary belief can no longer be experienced.

Topic: *Relationships*

A	Grumpy	M
B	Hard	M
C	Take time	G
D	Good sometimes	K
E	Rough	B
F	**Crafty**	**I**
G	Enjoyable	D
H	**Never last**	**K**
I	**Always problems**	**M**
J	Hidden agendas	F
K	**Love**	**H**
L	Not much love	F
M	**Difficult**	**F**

For this topic, **"Relationships"**, the client can be seen to have two separate belief structures held for the one topic. One has primary beliefs of **H-K** and the other belief structure has primary beliefs of **F-I-M**. This often occurs and is not an indication that the process has been completed incorrectly. All other beliefs that attach themselves to any of the primary beliefs such as J or L are classed as secondary beliefs and can only survive while the primary belief that sustains them exists.

On the following page we have set out the format which should be used when carrying out a GOLD Counselling session. It is permitted to photocopy this, as many as are required, or to prepare your own identical format.

> **"The advantages of using a model that can be actually played with or visualised are great when compared with mere description. A description only looks at one way of looking at something; it describes what is noticed at the moment. A physical model, however, contains all that could be noticed at any time; it includes all the possible ways of looking at the situation."**

> Edward de Bono
> *The Mechanism of Mind*

The GOLD Counsellors Association® topic list

TOPIC:

A ....

B ....

C ....

D ....

E ....

F ....

G ....

H ....

I ....

J ....

K ....

L ....

M ....

N ....

O ....

P ....

Q ....

R ....

S ....

T ....

U ....

V ....

13.5 Constructing the belief map

Once your client has created his list of items and identified to which item each is connected, it is then possible to construct a map of his belief structure.

This structure will, in a pictorial manner, set out exactly how each and every thought related to the selected topic is linked together. In doing so, it will also identify which beliefs are primary beliefs and which are secondary beliefs. To do this, one connects by arrows each of the related beliefs, ensuring that the arrow indicates the direction of flow of each belief from one to another. Once this belief map has been created it is possible to identify where problem areas exist and which beliefs are the primary beliefs – those which underpin the whole belief structure.

Once you have created this belief structure you can begin to understand exactly why the client has what he considers to be his "problem". In reality, it is his unconscious mind working artfully and simply to fulfil his beliefs.

The belief map below was created from the thoughts presented by the client for the topic **"Relationships"**.

Topic: *Relationships*

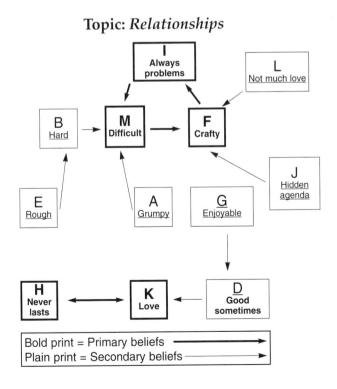

14. How Can Beliefs Be Changed?

14.1 Overview

As discussed in Chapter 3, so many people feel that once they've learned to behave, do, or think in a certain way, it is impossible to change. Well, they are right. That feeling they have is in itself a belief. Unless that can be changed, they won't change. To change a belief, we first need to understand what we believe now and where this belief came from.

GOLD Counselling works because with it you can use the only approach which will facilitate permanent change. What needs to happen is that we trace the thoughts in the client's mind back to the source of the problem. Once there we are then able to identify the specific piece of false reasoning, which persuaded him to believe that he should act or think in a certain way. You will always find corrupted information at the centre of any restricting or limiting beliefs. On correcting this corruption, either by removal or redesign, change will always occur.

> When working with a client's beliefs, it is the client's belief system itself which must change in order for the desired change to happen.

> The only way that this can happen is by your discovering what your client's beliefs are, NOW.

> The objective is to break the cycle with the least amount of discomfort to your client. It is therefore unnecessary to work only with the most traumatic belief. Look for the weakest link in the client's belief cycle to break first.

14.2 The difference between perception and belief

Our minds can allow us to see only what we believe and, therefore, we cannot see what we don't believe. Have you ever been in the situation whereby you have attempted unsuccessfully to convince someone that he is wrong? All the various arguments which you put up are discounted or ignored by him; often he will make your views seem small and his own ideas more important. It's as if he just can't or won't listen or see your point of view.

Perceptions are not facts, they are only a reflection of the beliefs of the perceiver. However, we all tend to believe our senses and assume that they are never wrong.

To test this we have included two exercises for you to carry out.

Exercise 1.

Read the following sentence out loud twice.

> THE FINISHED FILES ARE THE RESULT OF YEARS OF SCIENTIFIC EXPERIENCE COMBINED WITH THE EXPERIENCE OF MANY YEARS

Now, without reference to the written words, ask yourself how many letter **Fs** were there in the sentence?

Then check by reading the sentence from the page again.

The answer is six. Many people hear the F in "of" and *believe* it is a letter V. This is how the filtering of beliefs causes us to miss information without realising it.

Exercise 2.

Read the following sentence out loud

Now re-read it backwards and notice the error.

14.3 Belief identification

The actual symptoms of the client's beliefs are always present in the here and now. The client's unconscious mind has no shame in upholding his beliefs. This fact can be used by the therapist to bring about change in his belief structure since the unconscious mind is proud of its ability to remember exactly when a belief was formed.

It is possible to imagine the unconscious mind as the ultimate civil service department. A copy of everything is taken, just in case, and then filed and counter-filed. This means that when questioned in the correct way, the unconscious mind will release all the information asked of it, with delight. The unconscious mind has no concept of what a conscience is or what a conscience does. It doesn't care how or why a belief was formed, it only knows that it was formed, in the past, and still needs to be fulfilled.

When using GOLD Counselling the client is directed to return to the **exact time** when, and place where, the belief was formed. When the client has returned to that moment in time it is then possible to recreate the original feeling or emotion attached to that belief. The therapist can then dissect and analyse the memory with the client to ascertain both the actual event and his interpretation of it. A change must occur here for permanent change to take effect in the now.

It is from this position where the event and the interpretation can be separated that one is able to show the client how to re-evaluate, reappraise and then restructure that original belief through the creation of a fresh belief.

It will usually be the case that a client's beliefs will change daily and, in doing so, will often appear to conflict. Perhaps in the morning he may feel sad but by lunchtime he has moved into being relaxed and feels happier in the latter part of the afternoon. Most people would put this purely down to the situation they are in at present. However, once armed with an understanding of the **cyclic nature of beliefs**, a therapist will be able to understand how this change in emotions is natural and expected.

Of course, what we want to do for our client is to reduce the amount of time he spends in the less comfortable and more limiting emotional states and correspondingly to increase the amount of time he spends in rewarding states.

When working with a client, the method to enable him to focus on a particular part of the cycle is to ask the question *"What are you feeling right now?"*. This will encourage him to identify his beliefs and enable us to access his belief cycle. It is important to focus him on the NOW moment so that he can identify existing beliefs and not either old beliefs or future desires.

Once we have identified the originating belief, we can then focus the client on pinpointing where and how the belief was first learned. This concept reinforces the idea of the belief structure as a living organism – growing and connecting to new beliefs as time moves on. Therapy can then be applied to eliminate key areas where a negative influence is at work.

The therapist can be imagined as acting like a professional gardener who has been commissioned to reorganise and totally redesign a significantly overgrown garden. He would not waste time just tidying up the edges. No, he needs to quickly find the most powerful, most damaging weeds and plants and remove these, roots as well, so that they will no longer influence the way in which the garden grows ever again. And this is what the therapist can do with GOLD Counselling techniques.

14.4 Process overview

GOLD Counselling techniques make it simple for the therapist to identify problem areas and to effect changes easily and without any detrimental effects on the client. This can be achieved by:

- identifying the appropriate place in the belief structure to attach the new belief

- installing the new belief using the least amount of energy required

New beliefs can be installed in the client's unconscious mind using various techniques because the unconscious mind will seek to find an answer to any and all questions, be they real or imagined. The therapist can restructure a belief using the following approaches:

- by posing a question to the client which encourages his own examination of his belief

- by the creation of a new belief

- via a positively-worded suggestion

- by encouraging the client to play with thoughts and ideas in his mind

- by exploring the semantics of exactly who did what, who said what and who was actually responsible for the experience

15. Identifying The Belief Source

15.1 Key points to remember when restructuring beliefs

The beliefs which your client has mapped out on the paper in front of you may have existed for many years. In addition, every thought will have a level of emotion attached, some weak, some extremely powerful. Furthermore, we must recognise that many of these beliefs may be extremely useful and empowering, but they have become attached to other negative and limiting beliefs. Therefore, before you attempt to restructure any beliefs, you should understand the following points about the process of carrying out belief restructuring:

- it is important to correct any conflicting belief loops in your client's map of beliefs which may be causing confusion – although sometimes merely the revisitation of the memory causes the necessary change

- always correct primary beliefs

- always correct the most detrimental primary belief in a loop by evaluating its secondary beliefs

- eliminate beliefs which are detrimental to the success of therapy first (e.g. failure or worthlessness)

- the elimination of one belief will naturally explode the other or others related to it in the belief loop

- ensure that the nub of the problem is correctly pinpointed before starting to restructure beliefs (i.e. change the problem, not the symptom)

- recognise the significance of saturating the unconscious mind with the existing belief – the client must be totally absorbed in the question

- check to see if there are other beliefs supporting the original as a belief may be learned on more than one occasion

- always bear in mind the fact that nature hates vacuums and it is, therefore, important to reconstruct and/or fill the gap created by the review of beliefs

- conversely, the mind may appear to lose unimportant memories when there is no high emotional content contained within the belief cell

- consider carefully the links between major complexes before starting to restructure beliefs in order to be able to see the complete picture

- when dealing with a complex of highly-sensitive material, start by restructuring the least serious belief first in terms of emotional content

- be sensitive to potentially high-anxiety material in your client's lists (e.g. items such as "fear" and the name of a family member closely connected may indicate repressions of child abuse)

- recognise that a client may unconsciously be resisting or avoiding change

- look for ways in which a client links items on the list so as to ensure absolute free association of ideas (i.e. check for logical connections indicating that this is what he wants to believe or feels he should believe)

- ensure that a client creates a list of beliefs in the present tense in order to capture **NOW** moment beliefs

Provided that the therapist is mindful of these points he will be able to assist the client in locating the central core of the beliefs which underpin his problem. This will be direct and accurate and will ignore any peripheral issues surrounding the problem, and any erroneous associations or memories which the client falsely believes are the originating causes.

15.2 Belief restructuring techniques

The GOLD Counselling techniques contained herein will enable a therapist to assist clients to correct a limiting or inappropriate belief and install
a positive belief in its place. This is achievable by taking your client
through the following process:

1. Enter a state of rapport with your client, directing him to relax himself
   and let go of any tensions he may have – mental or physical.

2. Facilitate in him simple breathing techniques so as to allow him to
   focus on his internal experiences.

3. Ask your client to repeat to himself in the first person the selected
   question.

4. Ask him to repeat the question again and again, altering your voice
   tone and inflection with the prime objective of flooding and tiring his
   unconscious mind with the question.

5. Ask him to identify when, where and how the belief was first formed.

6. Regress your client to that specific point in his life when the existing
   belief was first formed.

7. Establish that the belief was formed at an earlier or inappropriate time
   in your client's life.

8. Verify that the belief was formed for the wrong reasons (e.g. a belief
   held erroneously by an authority figure).

9. Ask your client to identify and experience subsequent events whose
   outcomes had been shaped by the earlier belief.

10. Ask your client to acknowledge now that the negative belief is no
    longer necessary, feasible or appropriate.

11. Ask your client to imagine how the future would be if the new belief
    were installed.

There will be certain circumstances in which more complex belief-restruc-
turing techniques will be required. These techniques include:

1. developing new beliefs for a client who has no previous blueprint in his earlier life with which to form a positive belief – the new belief will need to be installed and fixed to an existing belief and then tested

2. dealing with complex beliefs which form a large loop

3. working with a client who has a number of belief complexes and each of these is inter-related.

15.3 The need to tire the mind

The unconscious mind has within it the information we need to locate where and when a belief was first formed. However, it may be unwilling to present this information to us. First we must tire it, through focusing the whole of the mind on one particular issue. By repeating again and again the particular belief, posed as a question, the unconscious mind will be forced to flow back in time to the originating place. Without this tiring effect, the mind will either present a recent incident, one of the secondary beliefs, or even produce something unrelated, acting as a screen for the original event. It is only through tiring the mind that we can quickly ascertain the originating cause of the belief. The ego protects beliefs so it is the ego that needs to be commanded to reveal the source of the belief. This it can also do without any resistance if the process is explained correctly.

15.4 Finding the belief source

Before a therapist carries out a GOLD Counselling analysis, he must ensure that he prepares a thorough case history of the client. This is to ensure that he can determine whether the symptom being presented can be worked on initially or whether there is a deeper issue which should be addressed first. For example, if the client has had a history of visiting various therapists, all unsuccessful, an analysis of the beliefs surrounding **"Failure"** would be an essential first step, to eliminate the secondary gain currently being fulfilled.

Once the belief structure map has been created, your next objective will be to determine which of the thoughts within the structure need to be revised so that new learning and understandings can take place.

When obtaining your client's focus on his beliefs, it is essential that your language is precise. Where possible always use the first person singular (e.g. ***"Where did I learn to believe the belief that I... ?"***) and, where possible, always use exactly the same words as those appearing on the GOLD Counselling topic list. Your objective will be to saturate your client's mind, to the total exclusion of everything else, with his existing belief and ask him to follow you in repeating the specific question again and again in his own mind in order to ensure that the precise source is identified.

A typical way of preparing your client to identify a limiting or inappropriate belief might be to begin by saying to him (while keeping rapport):

Therapist: *And as you relax there … calm and relaxed … just allow your body now … to discover that place of comfort there … inviting those arms and legs … those hands and feet … to release those tensions now … and you can be proud of your mind … constantly fulfilling all your beliefs … never questioning … just doing … only obeying … your faithful servant … and perhaps now you may want to know when and where you learned to believe that you believe that…*

Depending on the actual belief which your client needs to focus on, one of the phrases, such as those listed below, would be appropriate:

Where/when/how did I learn to believe the belief Relationships, bad?

Where/when/how did I learn to believe that I believe…

Where/when/how did I learn to believe the belief…

Where/when/how did I learn the belief that I believe…

Where/when/how did I learn that I believe…

Let your mind take you to that time, that place where I first learned to believe that I believe…

Where/when/how did I learn to believe the belief leg pain, loneliness?

When did I learn to believe that I was (ability/feeling) in (situation)…

When directing your client to consume his mind with this question, the client should adopt a relaxed pose, sitting or lying down and with his eyes closed. Some clients, however, will not feel comfortable closing their eyes. In these situations, simply pose the following question:

What do you see yourself doing? Tell me about that learning.

In many cases, a therapist will find that just the act of posing the question will provoke a profound emotional reaction within the client (this is known as an *abreaction*). This abreaction may take as many different forms as there are different ways to experience something emotionally. This could include tears, shouting, body shaking or coldness.

15.5 Identifying the beliefs to change

Once you have constructed the belief structure it is appropriate to explain to the client how his unconscious mind is operating via his ego to fulfil his beliefs. This will often be the first time that he will have consciously been aware of this process. With GOLD Counselling it is possible for one to actually see how the beliefs we hold are connected together.

Sometimes a client will attempt to justify why he wrote certain things or endeavour to change what he meant. Rather than become involved in an analytical discussion with the client about what has been written, it is important to delve deeper into the unconscious meanings. This is where having an understanding of what the words mean becomes important. All the beliefs identified during a GOLD Counselling session are derived from different experiences. Beliefs will contain information such as:

- **modality** – that is, visual, auditory, kinaesthetic, olfactory, gustatory

- **age** – simple language indicating childhood learning, more complex language originating from adulthood

- **organ language** – words trapped within the body indicating the source of the problem

- **double negatives** – unconsciously meaning the opposite of what the client believes is written

- **quotations** – comments or commands from family

- **ego** – the use of "I" when the belief is someone else's

- **slips of the pen** – and apparently inappropriate words

- **tense-mixtures** – phrases containing past and current tense.

The realisation which comes when we stop to acknowledge how we think, feel and the way in which we feel can be very emotional. Even just acknowledging that we have held on to these thoughts in the past is enough to begin the process of change. However, the skill of the counsellor is to identify which of the different beliefs should be operated on first.

The beliefs which are held need to be reviewed and classified into two broad types – useful or limiting. If it is unclear as to how a belief operates, ask the client. It is essential that you interpret his world from his viewpoint and not from your own. As GOLD Counsellors our aim should be to remove the limiting beliefs and, in doing so, to enable the client to experience his world in a different and more useful way. One should always leave the client in a more resourceful state and, therefore, once we have removed the limiting primary beliefs it may be necessary to introduce into the belief structure fresh ones.

One will usually need to revise one or more of the primary beliefs. Depending on the belief structure, however, it may also be necessary to restructure one or more of the secondary beliefs. This can be because of the level of emotion attached to the primary beliefs. In changing the secondary beliefs first, one is redirecting energy away from the centre of the belief structure and enabling those beliefs underpinning the whole structure to be questioned and changed.

When identifying the beliefs to be worked on, consider the following:

- correct any beliefs where there is conflict between two or more beliefs – this will be causing the client to expend an inordinate amount of energy trying to go in two directions at once

- always correct primary beliefs

- select the most detrimental primary belief by evaluating the secondary beliefs attached

- identify and remove any beliefs which would nullify the effects of therapy, such as failure or worthlessness

- ensure that the problem is actually addressed and not purely the symptom

- ensure that work is carried out on the earliest learning experience and not merely on a later supporting memory

- where the topic is highly emotional, commence work on the less sensitive beliefs first

- remember that your client's ego will attempt to sabotage the success of the process, although he will be unaware of this

- work on beliefs which your client actually believes, not on beliefs which he wants to believe

15.6 Dissecting the beliefs

In order for us to enable a client to begin to consider his beliefs from a different perspective, one must provide him with a way of recognising where the belief originated. While it may be clear to us that the belief which the client holds as his own was someone else's, the client's ego believes it is his. Therefore, any logical discussion about the matter will be unsuccessful. What is needed is a means which allows the client's unconscious mind once again to revisit the original thought from which the belief was created and, with the guidance of the GOLD Counsellor, to reinterpret and to recognise who really believed that belief.

The way this can be successfully achieved is in the use of questioning techniques. In order to answer a question, the client must access old memories. When this happens GOLD Counselling can enable the client to notice new elements of the original experience, elements which can shed a whole new interpretation on the original experience.

The questions which are employed need to be very precise so that we can focus on the precise root-cause of the belief. Once we have identified on which belief to work, an appropriate question based on the words contained within the belief needs to be constructed. This is done by taking the words of the belief and amending certain parts of the belief in order to express it in the current tense but not in the first person.

Let us look at some examples which reveal how we can amend the client's belief when we question it.

TOPIC	WRITTEN BELIEF	BELIEF TO QUESTION
Friends	I don't go out much anymore	Don't go out much
Work	I have to do everything around here	Have to do everything around here
Happiness	You don't care about how I feel	Don't care about, feel

It is clear that the way in which we use words when questioning beliefs has a totally different grammatical structure compared to that used in normal everyday speech. This is because we need to offer to the unconscious mind a very precise question about the original belief and this question must contain no more than the information which was sourced from that original belief. All the words around this core information have been subsequently added by the unconscious mind and the ego.

15.7 How to question a belief – identifying the source

The next step in the process of GOLD Counselling is to ask the client's unconscious mind to reveal where and when he first learned to believe his belief. During this process the client's ego will try to protect itself from having to change and, therefore, unless a very precise methodology is applied, the originating cause of the belief will stay hidden.

Once we have identified the belief to be worked on and stripped out any unwanted words, we can then begin the process of questioning the belief. This should be carried out while your client is in a state of centred and focused relaxation. Once he is in this state you should ask him to repeat to himself, again and again, with his own inner voice, a question constructed from the topic and the belief. This will usually take one of the following formats:

Where did I first learn to believe the belief – TOPIC – BELIEF?

When did I first learn to believe the belief – TOPIC – BELIEF?

Where was I when I first learned to believe the belief – TOPIC – BELIEF?

How did I first learn to believe the belief – TOPIC – BELIEF?

What happened so that I first learned to believe the belief – TOPIC – BELIEF?

Under what circumstances did I learn to believe that I believe that – TOPIC – BELIEF?

When asking the client this question, the GOLD Counsellor must pause at each of the dashes, separating the question into three parts. This has the effect of powerfully focusing the unconscious mind on the question. When repeating the question, the client must use an identical word-structure while, at the same time, injecting variety in pace, tone and inflection. The question must be repeated again and again for about ten to thirty seconds in order to tire the conscious mind. This eventually causes the ego to give up its protective hold on the original belief allowing it to be revealed. As the conscious mind tires, a feeling similar to boredom washes over the client – this is natural and indicates that one is closing in on the original memory.

This approach can be used to identify the originating cause of a belief, even where the belief has been expressed only as a colour, a feeling or a sound. For example:

Where did I learn to believe the belief – FEAR – GREEN?

In this way the association between the colour and the feeling will be identified.

Once the client has repeated the question to himself for ten to thirty seconds, the GOLD Counsellor then orients him with a further question such as:

What do you see yourself doing?
What is happening?
Where are you?
Tell me what is occurring?
What are you experiencing?

What happens then is that the client will find himself unconsciously taken back to an earlier experience from which the belief may well have been formed. We can then determine whether this was the place where the belief was formed by asking the client to ask himself the following question:

…and let your unconscious mind take you back to an earlier time, an earlier time when you first learned to believe the belief – TOPIC – BELIEF.

The client will either find that his unconscious mind will guide him to an even earlier experience or it fixates on the one presently being remembered – indicating that this is the originating experience. Sometimes a client may say that he cannot remember a particular experience and all he is experiencing is a general learning over a period of time. This can still be worked with since this is what his unconscious mind is letting him experience. It may be, however, that the client is resisting the acceptance of the memory from which the belief was formed – so you may need to ask him whether he does, in fact, wish to change. Provided all is in order, it is possible to continue with just this general learning instead of with a specific memory.

15.8 Reworking the belief

Once we have assisted the client in returning to the originating experience from which the belief was formed, we must now ask him to re-experience this memory in order to reinterpret it with fresh understanding.

The GOLD Counsellor should ask the client to describe what is happening. It is important to slowly develop the memory, adding details piece by piece, instead of briefly skimming through the experience, as would be preferred by the client's unconscious mind. This can take anything from a few seconds to a few minutes, depending on the amount of resistance the client's unconscious mind is using to protect itself from a new understanding.

The GOLD Counsellor must use his language skills to ensure that the client re-experiences the original situation as himself there and then and not as an observer. This will ensure that he feels the feelings which were experienced then and are still held within his body.

Once the client has verbalised what is happening and what he is experiencing, the GOLD Counsellor can then begin to ask more questions to assist the client in finding out who really believed the belief that the client thinks is his own.

Consider an example from a topic list on the subject of Learning. A primary belief was:

I am stupid.

When asked where the client had learned to believe this, his unconscious mind returned him to a schoolroom where he was told off by a teacher for getting something wrong. The teacher said:

You don't know that? You're stupid!

This caused so much embarrassment to the client that he had always felt stupid thereafter.

When this happens and the client finds himself back in the original situation as if he were still that age, any hidden feelings or thoughts from that memory will reveal themselves. This can take the form of tears, rage, anger, shouting or many other discharge-routes. These feelings which are being discharged will have been unconsciously related to the symptoms as experienced by the client. Once the discharge has occurred the symptoms will dissipate.

Once this has happened the GOLD Counsellor can move on to guide the client to understand who actually held the belief. This can take the following format:

Therapist: *So if I am hearing you correctly, I am hearing you say that Y is (saying/doing)?*

Client: *That's right.*

Therapist: *So if I am hearing you correctly, what I am hearing you say is that you believe that Y believed (belief)?*

Pause while the unconscious mind accepts a new view.

Client: *Yes.*

From this point onwards the client's unconscious mind has accepted the difference between the old thought of the client believing the original belief and the new thought that someone else really believed it. Then the client is free to consider and accept totally fresh beliefs.

This difference in viewpoint can be further enhanced by additional questions such as:

So would you treat a child in that way?
Is that a fair way to act?

How would you, as an adult, act if you saw another adult do that to a child?
What kind of person would do that?
Would you do that to someone else?
What is the purpose of a teacher?
What is the purpose of going to school?
What are you learning from teacher's actions?
What is this person projecting?

These questions act to further distance the client from the belief held by the other person. This works because the client can now reason and assess the original experience from an adult perspective and now have new insights which were not available to him when he was younger.

Occasionally someone may not be able to or be ready to acknowledge where a certain limiting emotion, such as guilt, came from. Perhaps it may be that he is not yet ready to acknowledge how someone else important to him has treated him in the past. If this happens when using GOLD Counselling, it is still possible to stop the belief of being guilty from continuing to permeate his everyday experiences. The following example shows how the therapist can use trance-logic to install a date-and-time stamp on the original memory to stop it from continuing to influence the client.

Therapist: *So if I am hearing you right, I am hearing you believe that you believe you should feel guilty for getting the maths test wrong?*

Client: *Yes.*

Therapist: *So as a seven-year-old girl, in that classroom, in that school, on that day, you felt guilty for getting that maths test wrong, back then?*

Client: *Yes.*

In applying this trance-logic to the client's memory, we have ensured that he only associates guilt with that one experience in the past. Therefore, he will feel guilty only if he were to become seven years old again and fail another maths test in that classroom. Clearly, as this is not possible, we have, therefore, succeeded in eliminating the ongoing belief about guilt. Furthermore, he will no longer see himself as guilty in other situations in the future.

15.9 Multiple-learning points

As discussed previously, the objective of GOLD Counselling is to take the client back to the original memory so that he can understand what the specific learning was back then. Normally there will be one profound learning from a single memory but there will sometimes be instances where the experience was so profound that two or more beliefs were created from it.

This means that the client will have this memory in more than one belief structure. At the time of the incident, the intensity of emotions which were released (or possibly are still repressed) caused the mind, in effect, to create multiple copies of the memory and to record them in different belief structures.

This is the reason why, if you were to take a client through a sequence of GOLD Counselling sessions, memories that had been discharged from earlier topics may appear in later ones. This does not mean your previous sessions were unsuccessful; it only means you have now unearthed a multiple-learning point.

For example, a boy was scolded and kept in after producing school results below the expectations of his parents. The two beliefs which he formed from this event were *"I am stupid"* and *"I am no good"*. Your client would benefit from reorganising both of these limiting beliefs. However, unless both appeared in one map you would not realise that the same incident was supporting two or more beliefs.

15.10 Cumulative-learning points

When asked to focus his mind back to the specific when he first learned to believe the belief, most clients will be able to locate the appropriate memory. However, in some instances, a client will respond that there is no specific memory, more a feeling of knowing this – the belief having been built up over a long time. We would always recommend that, as the therapist, you should aim to uncover the originating cause and since your client's unconscious mind has hidden away the original memory for a long time, you may need to push forcefully to enable it to reveal the truth. This is why the approach of tiring the mind through repeatedly asking it the same question is essential.

If your client still suggests that there is no particular or incident, go along with your client initially. "That's right, so just tell me anything that your mind chooses to show you " is one approach that, though surprisingly simple, can bring about a great deal of information.

Should the client continue to resist, stop the session momentarily. Ask him whether he understands the process and the importance of the work that he is doing. Check and be clear that he really does want to learn when and where he learned to believe the belief. Be compassionately forceful and assertive. Have in your mind that your objective should be to ultimately empower your client and not to perpetuate a belief that they are power-less.

Having said this, an analogy that may apply in this situation is of a patient going to see a dentist for a tooth extraction because they are unable to chew properly and therefore unable to enjoy their food. All is well until the dentist begins to extract the tooth whereupon the patient attempts to resist the dentist's help. Accept that your client in some cases would probably rather keep his problem instead of realising where it came from. It could be that there is a hidden agenda or that secondary gains outweigh the client's desired outcome. In any case respect your client's right to choose. The level of pressure applied to your client needs to be monitored carefully.

We would strongly recommended that you attend a GOLD Counselling practitioner training workshop if you are intending to work with clients who are suffering from deep-rooted emotional problems.

However, in situations where the client really cannot identify an originating memory, it is quite acceptable to work with the feeling that is being experienced by the client. The success of GOLD Counselling is in no way undermined by this occurrence. It is rather that the benefits to the client would be more profound if the original memory were revealed since we can then correct the exact incident, rather than purely the feeling based on his interpretations of the incident.

16. Eliminating Negative Beliefs

16.1 Methodology

Once you have facilitated in the client an understanding of where he first learned his belief, you have already carried out a significant piece of change-work. However, the process is not complete until the old belief no longer exerts any influence over the client.

At this stage your client will usually be in an altered state of awareness, very inwardly focused and extremely sensitive and suggestible to whatever you say. It is extremely important that you stay in rapport with your client, keeping him relaxed. Focus on using the specific words of your client, as identified on the GOLD Counselling topic list.

From this position the therapist must now determine how the belief became accepted as true by the client. This could have occurred in a variety of ways. To assist, we have detailed some examples below.

16.2 A belief formed by observation

Let us take as an example a client who is having relationship problems and has discovered that his primary belief was formed by watching his parents behave in a particularly argumentative way.

Therapist: *So if I am hearing you right, I am hearing you say that your mother and your father are fighting in the living room, then?*

Client: *Yes.*

Therapist: *So if I am hearing you right, what I am hearing you say is that you believe your parents believe that their marriage means arguments... then?*

Client: *(Pause, considering different viewpoint) Yes.*

Therapist: *So on that day, in that living room, back then…*

16.3 A belief formed by being told

In this instance, the GOLD Counselling topic sheet revealed that the client's primary belief was that he was told by another person *"I think I am stupid."*

Therapist: *So if I am hearing you right, Mr XX, your school teacher is saying that he believes you are stupid, then?*

Client: *Yes.*

Therapist: *So if I am hearing you right, what I am hearing you say is that you believe that Mr XX believes that you are stupid, then?*

Client: *(Pause, cognitive review of information) Yes.*

Therapist: *So on that day, in that classroom, back then...*

16.4 A belief formed by self-perception

For this client the GOLD Counselling topic list revealed that his primary belief was formed by self-perception and was *"I'm not a good person, I let people down"*.

Therapist: *So if I am hearing you right, I am hearing you say that you believe that on that day, at that time, when you were seven years old, you didn't stick up for your friend in the classroom?*

Client: *Yes.*

Therapist: *So if I am hearing you right, what I am hearing you say is that your friend didn't think that you stuck up for your friend, back then?*

Client: *(Pause, recognising difference) Yes.*

Therapist: *So on that day, when you were in that classroom, you believed that your friend believed ...*

Client: *Yes.*

There are many ways to continue from this point to provoke a perceptual shift of the original event. Listed below are some possible ways of proceeding.

Therapist: And if you could do something differently then, what would you like to have done that would make that different for you?

Therapist: And knowing what you know now what would you have done differently?

Therapist: So on that day you believed that "I'm not a good person, I let people down". And I wonder if your mind can remind you of other times that you have supported people.

Therapist: And I wonder if anyone has taught you to be supportive of your friends. And if you had not learned how would you know how to be supportive?

Therapist: And did you know that at that time then, your mind is behaving in ways that you could not control then, that's right, because if it perceives that, by you taking an action, then you could have put yourself at risk of harm? Your mind would stop you from taking that action then. Now that you have total control of your mind you can choose yourself.

17. Restructuring The Remaining Positive Beliefs

17.1 Overview

As discussed in Chapter 10, the unconscious mind will fulfil both positive and negative beliefs without question. *"I'm a failure"* and *"I'm successful"* are both appropriate and congruent beliefs within the unconscious mind, provided that it has stored away reference experiences to back these up.

While no-one would disagree that removal of the first belief would be beneficial, if the belief "I'm successful", were connected to "I'm a failure" after GOLD Counselling the removal of one belief would inevitably result in the loss of the other.

When reviewing a GOLD Counselling topic list, you will usually identify that positive beliefs are attached to negative beliefs. Following the elimination of the central negative belief, any useful beliefs attached to negative arms of the belief structure would slowly fade away.

What needs to happen in these cases is that the free-floating positive beliefs are then attached to the reset positive beliefs so as to form an even stronger reinforcement to the newly-formed attitude of mind.

17.2 The process of bridging beliefs

We must allow the client to consider the old negative belief in a way which permits his unconscious mind to construct a fresh, positive and liberating belief. Once this has occurred, his unconscious mind will reformat the belief structure into a totally different pattern. This structure will then exclude the previously-limiting primary beliefs and the connected, limiting secondary beliefs.

So that your client can accept the newly-formed beliefs, a therapist might ask a question phrased as follows:

What would there have to be in your mind, now, for you to believe that you believe that… ?

What would you need to believe in order to believe… ?

What would need to happen for me to believe that I believe that I… ?

…now, allow your unconscious mind to show you the effects of today's experience on the rest of your days from now…

If we work through the following example we can understand how this principle would be applied in practice. The client has produced a GOLD Counselling list on the topic **"Relationships"**.

Topic: *Relationships*

A	Happy	C
B	**Sad**	**H**
C	Good	G
D	Bad	B
E	Restricting	G
F	Fun	A
G	Manipulating	B
H	**Lonely**	**B**

Naturally, we will want to revise the limiting primary beliefs **B** *Sad* and **H** *Lonely*. Let us assume that this has now occurred. Unless we bridge the positive beliefs **A** *Happy*, **C** *Good* and **F** *Fun*, these will no longer be beliefs held in respect of relationships. To do this, we can pose the following style of question:

What do you need to believe to believe the belief Relationships, Good?

In answering this question your client will then have connected the belief to the new structure which was formed from the revision of the old, limiting primary belief.

The appropriate question can be identified by referring to the map produced from this topic list.

Relationships

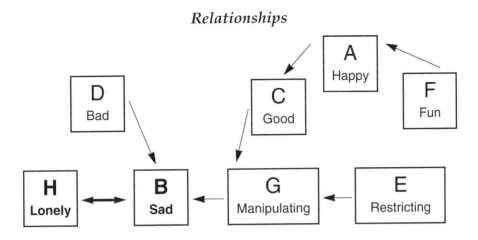

Bridging existing beliefs together

A client's list of beliefs on a topic, when connected and turned into a belief map, may consist of more than one structure. This is quite normal but it is usually found that a client's beliefs are not simply separated into one set of useful beliefs and one set of harmful beliefs. The way in which the beliefs are sorted is by energy. Therefore, if both a useful belief and a harmful belief have a large amount of energy in them, they will tend to connect together.

As GOLD Counsellors, therefore, we must recognise that in destroying a harmful belief, any connected useful beliefs will also be destroyed unless we can find a way to connect one useful belief to another useful belief either in another part of the same structure or to another belief structure. This can be achieved by asking the client:

What do I need to believe in order to believe the belief – TOPIC – BELIEF TO BE BRIDGED – BELIEF TO BRIDGE TO?

What would need to happen for me to believe that I believe that relationship, growth then unity, then growth then unity?

In using this strict format, the client's unconscious mind is forced to consider the strong, useful belief in the context of another useful belief causing the two to become connected in the mind.

17.3 Introducing new beliefs

How would you explain the concept of love to someone who has never felt love? How could someone who has never been happy understand what happiness is? If you did not know the words to use, how would you explain a feeling?

Questions similar to these will need to be answered by you when you work with some of your clients. This is because the belief structures which a client holds for some topics may consist purely of negative and limiting beliefs. Once he has let go of these beliefs, he will then be in a state of limbo. Without any positive or useful beliefs about the topic and without your guidance, this could result in his taking on more detrimental beliefs.

Within GOLD Counselling there exists a methodology which will, firstly, enable a client – who does not have any way to describe the positive, useful state he desires – to express himself and then to integrate fresh beliefs into a structure in order to reinforce the new state.

This procedure is known as *grafting* and can be used to enable a client, who does not know what the feeling he wants to have would feel like, to appreciate this feeling. With this technique the client can create this state in himself and then begin to recognise this state even more in his world on a day-to-day basis.

This can be achieved by asking the client to let his unconscious mind answer the following question:

Who do I know who would have the skills I now require?

Once the client is presented with this person, ask him to step into this person's body and experience just for a while being that person. When this happens you will usually notice psychological changes in the client. Then ask your client to drift back in time to the way in which he imagines that the other person experienced growing up. Ask him to identify how his parents and any brothers or sisters interacted with him. Then ask him to mentally walk himself through that other person's life, focusing on how the skills he wants have helped this other person in his life up until the present day.

The use of the imagination is greatly encouraged to help bring about new learning and insight. Also through role-play a client may wish to learn a new belief. Edward De Bono in his book *Conflicts* (Penguin) wrote:

If you role-play being a thinker you will become a thinker.

He goes on to say that:

In time it becomes a habit. In time you become the thinker you have tried to be.

Having completed this, then ask the client to step back into his own body, letting his unconscious mind take with him all the learning and insights required to enable him to believe his new belief. Once this is completed, the client will have integrated the new beliefs held by the other person into his own unconscious mind.

17.4 Overnight integration – the time effect

During our sleep, significant work is carried out by the unconscious mind in collating and sorting information based on our experiences of the previous day. Our mind always needs to connect new learning to old experiences, only ever revising old experiences if forced to. It is, therefore, essential that any restructuring is completed on the same day, or else the memories within your client's mind will change and will no longer support the beliefs as written on the belief map. This means that any work carried out at a later session based on the old map would not be as effective, since the thoughts and beliefs will have already been restructured.

At the instant when a client understands from where an original belief first came and then reworks this, significant change will begin to take place. Immediately after the realisation, some clients then have flashes of insight indicating why certain places, people or activities were important to them before.

In addition to this, change at an even more profound level will be taking place outside the client's conscious awareness. During the time we are asleep, our minds process all the experiences of the day – sifting and sorting these experiences in order to make meaning of them, in accordance with all the beliefs we hold as true. Since the day's learning contains significant changes for the client, his unconscious mind will, in effect, be reprogramming his ego. On waking the next day, he will most probably be unaware of any differences, since we all filter the world via our ego. If the ego has changed, the filter changes without our noticing it.

It is only when the ego is presented with old situations which had discom-forted it before that it may recognise the difference. Possibly if the client is undergoing a sequence of sessions with you he may mention that he feels different but that he is not sure why. Depending on the client's situation it may or it may not be appropriate to reveal how the change has occurred.

This change which is experienced by your client is perfectly natural. He will not recognise the change since he is now seeing the world through his beliefs and as his beliefs change, the way he sees the world will change. This Catch 22 syndrome means that he will probably not recognise that his original, presenting problem has dissipated and no longer troubles him. An analogy might be that of a computer being installed with a new program. On completion the computer asks to be turned off so that it can incorporate the new data.

18. Designing New Belief Systems

There are many reasons why someone comes to therapy. For our purposes, we will categorise these into three possibilities.

1   The client is having an experience which he does not want to have.

2   The client is not having an experience which he would like to have.

3   The client is having an experience which he would like to replace with another experience.

This chapter deals principally with clients in categories 2 and 3. With both of these categories, the client is seeking to alter or to expand his system in some way. Category 1 is seeking to stop something from happening and this is achieved in the usual way as described in other chapters in this book.

With clients in categories 2 and 3, we know that the change sought requires the client to have new ways of perceiving reality. If he were able to do so, then he would already be fulfilling his desire.

Before we can set out to help a client, we need to have a fairly good idea that the client has some desired outcome from therapy. Having clearly established the desired outcome with the client, we need to investigate his belief system to establish whether or not he has a circular belief system which would support his desired outcome. Should the client not have a belief system which fulfils the client's desired outcome, we would need to design such a system.

A GOLD Counselling topic list reveals much about what goes on in the client's mind and, therefore, what his perceptual experience of the world is. Significantly, a GOLD Counselling topic list also reveals what beliefs are not there. These are beliefs that are not in existence and would need to be designed and installed in accordance with the client's desired outcome. How can a client have some experience that is not a part of his own belief system?

We will show through examples the steps needed to design a belief system that would encapsulate and sustain the client's desires. This chapter may also highlight some of the reasons why affirmations may be a waste of time.

Let us look, firstly, at the example of a client who comes along for therapy because he feels that his marriage is not working. The client has already told us more than he realises. The client does not like the relationship in which he is in. For him to be able to tell us this, he must, on some level, know that there is an alternative or he would not be looking for one.

The following list reveals the circular reality the client is experiencing on the subject of "Marriage".

Topic: *Marriage*

A	Together	B
B	Forever	A
C	Trapped	A
D	Children	E
E	Responsible	F
F	No space	A
G	Pressure	C
H	Disagreements	G
I	Visitors	L
J	Mortgage	G
K	Boring	G
L	Must look right	G
M	Secrets	L
N	Keep going	M

Topic: *Marriage*

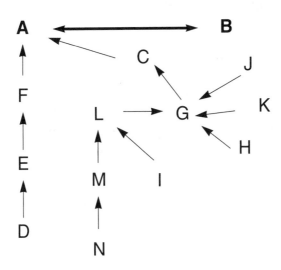

What we can see from the above list is that the client's current circular reality is disruptive, that unless there is a positive belief structure to build on, most efforts are likely to be fruitless. This list, having been restructured and negative beliefs neutralised, would not leave the client with much in the way of a model to build a belief system on. If left to the unconscious, it would fill the void with whatever remains to form a new belief system. Just a reminder at this point – the unconscious cannot accept voids, it has to fill the space which has been created. The client would have to investigate further to see what his unconscious has with which to fill that space. We would have to keep restructuring until a suitable belief system emerged. This would be quite a long, drawn-out way of getting there. The possibility of not getting there is also quite strong. This would be like saying that a blockage, which was causing water not to flow on to a field, has been unblocked and will rectify a problem and so now we should see growth. That would be fine if you have no preference as to what the field will yield. If, however, you want asparagus, then the land needs to be prepared for that and the right seeds need to be sown.

What we are proposing in this chapter is to allow the client to create a desired outcome which would be used as a design-model for the client's unconscious.

The following examples will show why – unless there already exists a positive structure to build on – efforts to build any lasting positive beliefs will probably last either only temporarily or fail.

When deciding to have a house designed, you could spend a great deal of time planning your needs for now and allowing room for expansion. Consideration would be given to the environment you live in and include such things as climate conditions, amount of sunlight, location, neighbours, etc. Having done this, we need to have an understanding of the ground conditions. Then the construction could proceed utilising the best available materials.

All the work that had gone into the design of the building could be wasted unless the builder used a site map and survey plan and had an understanding of the ground on which the house would be built. One needs to have a good idea of what can and cannot be built on this land. The land itself can be dredged and reclaimed. It can be altered in a way which would allow a house of this design to be built on it. In most cases, this can only be undertaken when the area has been cleared and made ready with the kind of foundations which would allow the construction of this type of building.

Primary beliefs are the foundations, the building blocks for such designs. Without such foundations, whatever is built either will inevitably collapse in a heap or will never get built at all. This would be a little like building sandcastles on the beach by the sea. They are there for a while, then the tide comes in and the rest is history. All the effort to build the house will be wasted. At best a great deal will be learned about how not to do it.

Often we meet with people who have spent a great deal of time and money, invested a great deal of energy, have made great commitments to self-improvement and still find themselves, years later, unable to make any significant improvements in their lives. Here we would say that no matter how hard this person tries to improve his life, without first clearing the area which he intends to build on, no change will occur and a great deal of time and energy will be wasted.

Similarly, before a farmer plants his harvest, he will prepare the land and remove any objects, such as large boulders, that are likely to prevent the production of his crop. As a point of interest, should the land which has been cleared be left unattended, it would begin to fill with whatever surrounds it. Nature fills voids. The examples we can give here are endless.

As with all building structures, you need to be confident that the foundations are correctly placed and sufficient in strength to sustain the structure that has been designed.

Once the building has begun, it could be dangerous to dig up at the footings and check to see if the footings are still holding. In doing this, one could, in effect, be weakening rather than strengthening them. So it is important to ensure that the foundations are right before commencement of any building works.

The design of the foundations needs to be such that they will support the structure and include expansion possibilities. What we are suggesting here is that once a building has been constructed, we need to ensure that sufficient consideration has been given for the volume of traffic which will flow. Also, we need to consider the installation of electrical appliances and the ever-increasing demands on the electrical system.

What we are talking about here is design. Without design, it is just a question of luck – just closing your eyes and hoping for the best. This is perhaps why, sometimes, therapy flounders. It is not that the therapy itself does not work but rather that it has not taken into consideration some of the finer details which would make it more effective.

Looking at the first example, we have a client's belief system showing us the beliefs he has on the subject of "Marriage". At a glance what we can see from the "Marriage" list is what the client's perception and experience of marriage is. The client is seeking help to understand and repair his perception of marriage. He feels that he is trapped and pressured in his marriage. The dismantling of the primary belief system would be a prerequisite to any new beliefs being installed. This is done through the methods mentioned in other chapters in the book.

As therapists, we need to determine which appropriate belief system to design and to develop further in order to fulfil the client's desired outcome. So, in effect, we need to ascertain what the client can perceive about marriage. This will enable us to see what foundations are needed and where they need to be placed to build a new belief system. This is an important point if we are to be effective in our work.

How this happens is really quite simple. In order to believe something, we need to perceive it. It matters not if what we perceive is visible only in others; the key is first to establish that the perception of the desire exists, albeit reflected in others. For, in order to recognise it in others, one must be able to perceive it initially. This applies to both constructive and destructive beliefs.

As far as the mental processes are concerned, it is worthwhile remembering that the unconscious mind does not understand positive and negative. All things within the unconscious mind just are. The mind gets pleasure from fulfilling beliefs, it does not judge the value of the belief. It just does. It does not think, it just does. It does not evaluate beliefs, it just fulfils them. It is up to the individual consciously to evaluate and re-evaluate beliefs.

In the example below of Client A, on the topic headed "What I desire in a relationship is", the client produced some very useful information to help us to establish what the client would like to have happen and what is possible.

How can you have something that you do not know exists? What we are suggesting here is that if you can extract from your client, at the very least, what he believes can and does exist, you are half way to helping him to achieve it.

In addition to a list of what exists in a client's belief system, a GOLD Counselling topic list can also be utilised to determine what the client cannot believe possible for himself. A list could be generated showing you, the therapist, another area of the client's mind where the client's disbeliefs exist. This list would be headed "I can't believe I can".

A "Desire" list will, in effect, reveal much more than the client is aware of. From the therapist's point of view, these lists will reveal not only what is possible but also where to employ the necessary energy to build a new belief structure, ensuring that it is built on a solid foundation. That is to say, the client will have revealed to you the foundations which would need to be in place in order that the work done during therapy will be supported by the client's unconscious mind. Otherwise, it will be like trying to mix oil and water. No amount of shaking will allow them to mix and blend into one.

What needs to happen from the therapist's point of view is for the therapist to get an understanding of the client's perception of what the desired outcome paradigm looks like. That is to say, a map of the client's desire. Also what key characteristics exist in the client's belief structure in the form of primary beliefs which need to be present in order for the therapist to incorporate them.

During the design stage, the client can be as demanding in his desire as he wants to be. There are no limitations other than that which has been put in place by the client. Suffice it to say that it would be completely inappropriate for the therapist to make any suggestions or recommendations to the client. An element of realism is called for, though. For example, someone having a desire to be an airline pilot is not a problem unless he has just passed his one-hundred-and-fifth birthday. Then he may have a problem in passing the medical.

We are being shown by the client's unconscious mind what foundations would need to be altered. A little like a car showing you where the mounting blocks need to be placed for the engine to be supported.

Let us look at a list generated by the client – who had created the previous list on "Marriage" – on the topic of "What I desire in a relationship is".

Topic: *What I desire in a relationship is (client A)*

A	Happiness	J
B	Sharing	D
C	Compassion	R
D	Growth	K
E	Family	K
F	Children	E
G	Love	M
H	Lovemaking	P
I	Play	J
J	Fun	I
K	Purpose	T
L	Autonomy	N
M	Caring	R
N	Encouragement	R

O Health   A

P Joy   D

Q Work   K

R Demonstrative   S

S Tactile   R

T Prosperity   D

Topic: *What I desire in a relationship is (client A)*

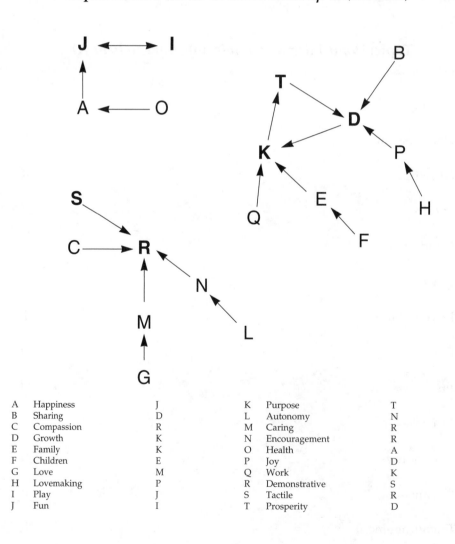

A	Happiness	J	K	Purpose	T
B	Sharing	D	L	Autonomy	N
C	Compassion	R	M	Caring	R
D	Growth	K	N	Encouragement	R
E	Family	K	O	Health	A
F	Children	E	P	Joy	D
G	Love	M	Q	Work	K
H	Lovemaking	P	R	Demonstrative	S
I	Play	J	S	Tactile	R
J	Fun	I	T	Prosperity	D

Example A shows that the client would need to have certain primary beliefs in place for him to have a fulfilling relationship, beliefs which he currently believes he does not have.

The following point is important to remember. So that the client can generate such a list, he would need to have perceived everything on that list. So we could say that the client's perception allows him to believe that it is possible to have these things. It may be that although he can perceive this, he may believe that he personally cannot achieve this but that others can.

Perhaps the client has some of the primary beliefs such as Play and Fun already in his life. Let us suppose that the client does not have Tactile and Demonstrative in his relationship. This raises several questions for us.

Firstly, can any other secondary beliefs exist without these two primary beliefs? As far as the mind is concerned, in our opinion, this would not be possible. The building blocks would have no foundations on which to build.

The client's mind has shown us what primary beliefs need to be in place for these beliefs to take root. It may seem a little complicated at first. Let us explain with a little more detail and further examples.

Topic: *What I desire in a relationship is (client B)*

A	Friends	F
B	Buddies	E
C	Sex/Lovemaking	N
D	Sharing	L
E	Togetherness	F
F	Soul mates	M
G	No secrets	H
H	Open	B
I	Strong	F

J	Sharing hobbies	L
K	Touch	N
L	Time together	D
M	Companions	D
N	Expressive	C

Topic: *What I desire in a relationship is (client B)*

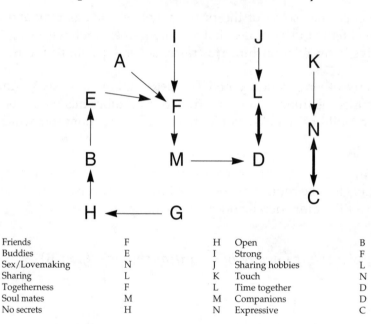

A	Friends	F	H	Open	B
B	Buddies	E	I	Strong	F
C	Sex/Lovemaking	N	J	Sharing hobbies	L
D	Sharing	L	K	Touch	N
E	Togetherness	F	L	Time together	D
F	Soul mates	M	M	Companions	D
G	No secrets	H	N	Expressive	C

We can see from the list generated by client B that there would need to be Sharing (D) and Time together (L) in one belief system and Expressive (N) and Sex/Lovemaking (C) in a second belief system for the client's belief and his desired outcome to manifest itself in his life.

When compared to client A, who requires Tactile (S) and Demonstrative (R) in one circular reality and Fun (J) and Play (I) in a second with Prosperity (T), Growth (D) and Purpose (K) in the third, we can see that the focus of attention will need to be very different for each client if we are to help fulfil the desires of each client.

What we can deduce from this is that by applying design A to client B, we would not bring about the desired outcome for client B. Similarly, if we were using a map of Australia, it would not allow us to travel around

Germany. If anything, it is likely to confuse the traveller. Perhaps even to keep him lost forever.

From this point on we will, subject to having neutralised any negative beliefs, be working with both clients in a similar way. We have discovered the beliefs that need to exist in each client and all that remains is to instil these beliefs.

The process of instilling new beliefs requires the therapist to be imaginative and creative in his/her approach. The human imagination is a profound gift and can be utilised to its fullest form to fulfil the client's needs. The process requires the client to be asked the following in the most appropriate way:

Example from client A

Therapist: *Where did I learn to believe that I believe "Relationship Fun"?*

Client: *Nothing comes to mind.*

Therapist: *So how do you know what it is to have "Relationship Fun"?*

Client: *My mind is reminding me that my Uncle and Auntie were always having fun when we played together. They were always playing around. He used to chase my Auntie around and they would both be giggling and laughing together. It was fun to watch them be like that.*

Therapist: *How does that feel to watch them there now… then?*

Client: *It's a good feeling that makes me want to laugh. It's funny she's splashing water on him in the garden.*

Therapist: *And what would need to happen for your mind to learn that this is the right way to be in a relationship so that "Relationship Fun"?*

Client: *I would need to feel that I'm having fun in a relationship. It's interesting because I had forgotten how much fun I used to have with my Uncle and Aunt. I suppose I just need to have that feeling.*

Therapist: *And would you like to have your mind learn how to have that feeling?*

Client: *Yes.*

Therapist: Now then, can you allow your imagination to do something for your mind which would allow your mind to do something for you?

Client: Yes.

Therapist: I know you know that your mind stores everything you learn... now... I wonder if... you know that your mind can also learn from your imagination. So what I would like you to do is to see your Uncle there, then, in your mind now and imagine what it feels like to be him for a while and just pretend, if you like, to be playing there in the garden and having fun.

The client can be encouraged to magnify the feeling of fun and slowly to transfer those feelings into his adult life. This can be achieved by asking the client to imagine or to think what would need to happen or what he would need to do in order to instigate Relationship Fun in his life. It would also be possible to use well-formedness criteria in order to further the client's desired outcome.

The therapist would approach each desired primary belief and work to procure from the client's mind where the client had first seen or experienced this feeling or behavioural pattern.

Where no memory is forthcoming from the client's unconscious, we can utilise the client's imagination and ask him to imagine a situation which would fulfil his belief. On occasion, clients who are having difficulty with this would be invited to recall a film or a video which contained a scene with the appropriate belief or feeling. The client would be asked to step into second position and experience what he is seeing. This has proved particularly useful with clients who have few resources of their own to call upon.

At all times, keep in mind that the desired primary belief should be the goal in your treatment strategy.

19. "I Can't" Idiom – Negative Restructuring

As in the chapter on design paradigm, this chapter shows that while a great deal of work can be accomplished with a client by restructuring disruptive beliefs, a therapist can never be sure whether there are any other structures which are concealed in the fabric of the client's psyche. Beliefs are inter-linked on so many levels that often a very thorough investigation is needed.

A great deal can be achieved by extracting from a client a belief list headed "I believe I can't". This is particularly useful if the client, having exhausted the more common topics, still finds himself unable to fulfil his desired outcome. In order to be able to write such a list one must be able to perceive the very thing which the client believes he cannot achieve.

Constructing a GOLD Counselling topic list on a negative subject can be a little more difficult to link than a regular GOLD Counselling topic list, because you will be asking the client to link one negative thought to another.

The following example on a "I can't believe I" list produced a wealth of knowledge which the client had but did not know he had. What we are saying here is that when the client is telling you what he cannot achieve, he is also telling you what he can perceive, even if it is not for himself. This approach to resolving conflicts can be a little surprising when a therapist has been working with a client for a while, believing that the client has overcome difficulties and is on the path to fulfilling his desired outcome, only to discover that there is still something outstanding after a few weeks.

Topic: *"I can't believe I"*

A	Can be happy	J
B	Can make it	M
C	Can let go	F
D	Am worth it	H
E	Will find myself	K
F	Can be without suffering	A
G	Am strong	M
H	Have a personality	T
I	Will succeed	M
J	Will find my alter ego	A
K	Can find my destiny	R
L	Will get out of my present state	B
M	Can be free	K
N	Will be able to forgive	C
O	Am like others	P
P	Am a pessimist	O
Q	Can fulfil my potential	P
R	Can fulfil my dreams	K
S	Can find the right way	E
T	Can make my mind up	H
U	Can commit	A

Topic: *"I can't believe I"*

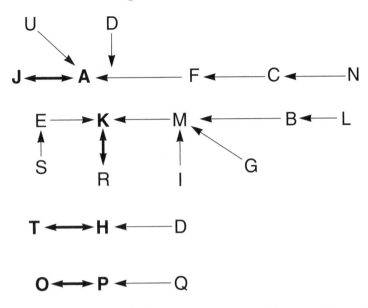

The client was asked the following question *"Where am I learning to believe that I believe I believe – can't be happy?"* This question was asked several times and the client was given time to allow his unconscious mind to reveal the place of learning.

The client found himself in a room with his mother sewing. Apparently this was something which was not uncommon. It appears that the client spent time copying his mother's hobby. The client then recalls thinking how sad he felt that his mother was. We continued to search his mind and what his mind was learning at the time. The client recognised that his mother being sad disabled him from being happy. The client revealed that his mother cannot be happy and continued to recall that she has never been happy.

Therapist: So if am hearing you right, I'm hearing you say that you believe that your mother can't be happy?

Client: Yes.

Therapist: And I believe you when you say to me that you believe that your mother can't be happy there then.

The client was asked to explore what his feelings are at that moment. It transpired that the client was feeling content sitting there and it was only the realisation of his mother's sadness that generated the thought that created the feeling "Can't be happy".

By breaking this belief cycle, the client no longer had the belief that he cannot be happy. Having resolved this, the client was encouraged to discover a time and a place when he was happy then. The session continued with the client finding several happy memories.

This method employed – using "I believe I can't" – can be extended to more specific subjects such as "I can't believe relationships are", "I can't believe work can be", "I can't believe I can be wealthy" and so on. At all times, precede the question with "Where did I learn to believe that?"

20. Overcoming Difficulties

Certain considerations need to be taken into account with some primary beliefs before commencing to search for the origin of the belief.

There are times, when working with a client's belief list, when you will come across what appears to be a difficulty or an impasse. That is to say, it may seem that the client is not able to find the source of the belief. It may seem that no matter how hard your client and you, the therapist, search to find the belief, you are met with what appears to be resistance, client non-compliance or even a doubt of the whole process.

We are not suggesting that the former is not a possibility but there are some other considerations to take into account.

Let us examine some possibilities.

Possible outcomes and overcoming strategies

1. *The client has insufficient understanding of the process*
Be clear in your explanation to your client about what is expected of him. Also ensure that you have a clear understanding of your client's expectations.

2. *The client has a higher-order anxiety in force which needs to be dealt with first*
Using your own preferred method of eliciting information from your client, ensure that what the client wants to have happen is not in direct conflict with what he wishes to achieve with you. So that if you are working with a client who wants to be able to pass his examinations, be sure that on his "I am" list he is not seeing himself as not good enough.

3. *The client has a fear of failure, fear of success or a failure-syndrome*
The client who will sabotage the whole process by not complying with your request to complete lists and even forgets to bring them, may well be fulfilling a belief that he is a failure and he will do whatever is necessary to fail at his therapy. This can also apply to a client who has a fear of success and even one who has a failure-syndrome. Take time to assess with which belief systems you are going to work, so that you can minimise the risk of activating a failure. Alternatively, remove any belief which may lead to failure initially.

4. *The client is trying too hard*
The client is an over-achiever and is putting too much pressure on himself. Take the time to ensure that you explain that the process requires a relaxed yet focused mind.

5. *The client's outcome is not worth the cost*
The outcome is not worth the cost, time or effort expended by the client. This can be dealt with by using a well-formed outcome and ensuring that the client is clear about what is involved before you commence therapy.

6. *The client's symptoms are not recognised when presented in therapy*
This can be one of the more difficult problems to recognise simply because it is so obvious. As much as the client's mind has no problem in displaying the birth-place of a belief, it assumes that the information will be accepted literally and includes the symptoms attached to that belief.

This requires a fuller explanation in order to gain the necessary insight to help you and your client overcome this problem. We shall give a few examples at this point as a way of demonstrating how to approach the situation and how to overcome any difficulties.

It is important to be very aware of what the belief which you are seeking to alter is and how the belief and relevant symptoms manifest in the client. Therefore, the word which is being sought needs to be understood as well as what the word means to your client and also what symptoms the word carries with it for your client.

In the following example we are working with a client who has presented a list on the topic of "Disappointed". The essence of the list contained two primary beliefs. For the purposes of this exercise, we will be speaking only of the primary beliefs.

The primary beliefs in this cycle are "Can't understand it" leading to "Why?" This, if not recognised at the offset, could result in a never-ending circle of questioning, on the one hand, or an incomprehensible explanation, on the other. The whole process might be questioned unless time is taken to grasp what it is that is being sought.

We need to explore the information carefully in order to determine what needs to be found and how to bring about change, keeping in mind that the client's belief system seeks to fulfil "Disappointed". From the therapist's viewpoint. the questions which need answering in the client's mind are what is "It?" and "Why?"

Here we are seeking to find a time when the client was disappointed with an inability to understand the situation. Therefore, it is precisely that situation which will present itself in your session with your client. As far as the client's mind is concerned, it has learned to be disappointed and will, therefore, draw situations into his life in order to fulfil the belief that he is disappointed and will also leave the client not being able to understand why the situation came about. The symptoms will be apparent in your consulting room during your session.

In this example, the client finds himself recalling an image which did not make sense to him. It is important that you agree with the client that it does not make sense. Here follows an extract of the GOLD Counselling session.

Client: *I can't understand it.*

Therapist: *That's right, I can't understand it. Where is it – I can't understand it?*

Client: *I am just standing there.*

Therapist: *That's right, just standing there (pause), and what is it that is happening?*

Client   *They are just walking away.*

Therapist: *Now then, who is it that is just walking away?*

Client: *My uncles are just walking away.*

Therapist: *And what is it that happens to you when they are just walking away?*

Client: *I can't understand why.*

Therapist: *Why what?*

Client: *What I'm doing here.*

Therapist: *What I'm doing where?*

Client: *At the boarding school.*

Therapist: *What's happening there at the boarding school?*

Client: *They are just leaving me here. I can't understand what I'm doing here.*

Therapist: *And how does being left there feel?*

Client: *I feel sad (pause), disappointed that they are just leaving without me.*

Therapist: *And why is it that you have been left there at boarding school?*

Client: *Study, my Mum sent me here to study.*

Therapist: *That's right.*

The session revealed that the client at the age of seven years was sent to a boarding school in a different country and away from his mother. No adequate explanation was given as to why he had to go to a different country and could not stay at a local school like his cousins, friends, etc.

The symptoms of this learning (or belief) were that people would do things which he would not expect, nor be able to understand and he would be left disappointed. The client understood from the session that this was something which he experienced frequently.

There are words used by clients which need to be carefully considered. With the example above, the words "Why?" and "I can't understand it" in the client's belief structure meant that the client would never get an understanding and would always be searching for one. The mind continues to create the situation over and over again each time with a greater intensity with each cycle.

The task of GOLD Counselling is not only to establish that such a circular reality exists but also to help the client find the answer which he has been seeking. These types of beliefs need special consideration prior to commencement.

List	Belief	Possible Outcome	Suggested approach commence by agreeing **"That's right"**
Success	Illusive	I can't see anything	And if you could, what would you imagine and see now… then?
Exams	Stuck	Nothing's happening	And how is it when you move to when something is happening then?
Relationships	Frozen	Nothing's moving	And where are you when nothing's moving… then?
Relationship	Blank	Nothing's there	And where are you there with nothing there?
I am	Lost	I can't find anything	And find a moment and pause to allow that memory to come and find you now… then.
Relationship	Confused	It's confusing	And where are you when it's confusing, there then?
Work	Hard	Can't find anything	And how is it, there, with nothing to find… then.
Home	Locked out	Not getting anything	And how is it, there locked out, not getting anything… then?
I am	Secretive	There's nothing there	And where are you with nothing, there then?
Finishing	Bored	I can't do this	And what is it you won't do, there then?
Friends	Secret	I'm not seeing anything	And take a moment to let your mind unveil the secrets it contains… then.
Marriage	Divorce	I don't believe it	And what is it that you don't believe… then?
Sex	I don't know	I don't know	Where are you there when you don't know then?
Failure	Foggy	It's not clear	Let your mind clarify what's not clear then, and now tell me what happens… then.

137

The suggestions given above are by no means the only ways to approach the questions. The use of clear language would greatly enhance the effectiveness of GOLD Counselling.

Note that the client may respond to some of your questions from his memory. That is to say, he is in the moment. So you may find that questions, such as the example below, arise during the session.

Therapist: *That's right. And where are you with nothing there… then?*

Client: *Here.*

Therapist: *Where's here… then?*

Client: *I'm in the kitchen and Mum won't tell me where Dad has gone.*

Therapist: *That's right. And how is that for you – when Mum won't tell you where Dad has gone?*

The focus of attention needs to be on the word or the phrase that the client uses. Have an expectation that the client will reveal that he is at the right place. This the client will do by showing the symptoms of his beliefs. So that if the belief is "Confusion", then expect that the client will be confused by what he sees/hears/feels.

This also applies to physical symptoms such as headache, panic, feeling sick, shaking, dizziness, tightness, etc. What happens when a client experiences these types of effects is that he is recalling an event where he learned a particular feeling.

The following example may give you a clearer understanding of the release of physical belief.

A client in her mid-fifties came for therapy to deal with her panic attacks when she travels on an aeroplane, underground train or elevator. Her belief list on the topic of "Got to get out" – as this, she felt, was the most dominant thought – contained the following four primary beliefs in her cycle: "Can't get out", "Dark", "Can't breathe" and "Fear".

The client was questioned accordingly.

Therapist: *Where am I learning to believe that I believe "Got to get out… dark"?*

Client: *It is dark.*

Therapist: *That's right, dark.*

The client started to breathe with difficulty. Her breathing was becoming more and more pronounced. The client's right hand was moving and had a shape which looked as if she was holding a ball. She continued with her breathing getting tighter and the hand movement on the right hand becoming more pronounced and in what appeared to be a painful experience.

Therapist: *What's happening?*

Therapist: *Where are you when you want to get out?*

Client: *It's dark. I want to get out and the door won't open.*

Therapist: *What door won't open?*

Client: *I don't know, it's dark.*

Therapist: *What's stopping the door from opening?*

Client: *He's locked the door. Let me out.*

Therapist: *Which door has he locked?*

Client: *The coal-cellar door.*

The client, at this time, was quite distraught with a frightened expression, her hand was still moving trying to open the door, her breathing was erratic and she was repeating that she wanted to be let out.

Therapist: *What happens next?*

Client: *I'm in the kitchen. It's that boy from down the road, he locked me in.*

Therapist: *What's happening?*

Client: *He's run away.*

Therapist: *How are you now?*

Client: *I'm OK now.*

All the symptoms had now disappeared. The client was breathing normally and naturally. The hand movement had stopped and the client had a relieved expression on her face.

The client went on to say that it was exactly how she felt when she was anywhere in which she could not get out and all the same feelings which she experienced when flying.

We tested the results with some future pacing to see if there were any remaining symptoms. The session lasted approximately twenty-five minutes. The session was successfully completed.

Be aware during your sessions with your clients that their symptoms will reveal themselves to you. They may appear very subtly or with full force. What is certain is that they will appear.

21. Future Pacing

With GOLD Counselling you must first confirm, using the client's language exactly, what it was he learned to believe and from whom, where and when. Once the client has confirmed this, the therapist can then focus the client's mind on who it was that had, therefore, really held the belief in the past.

Once the client understands that the belief he believed was actually someone else's, a significant rearrangement in his belief structure will take place.

At this stage it is then appropriate to ask the client to review how this original incorrect learning has affected him since the originating time and up until the here and now. One method would be to suggest to him the following:

And you can allow your unconscious mind to start to show you the effects of that incident, there, then, on the rest of your life, up to now, as I count from 10 down to 1 ...10 ...9 ...8 ...7 ...6 ...5 ...4 ...3 ...2 ...1 ...that's right.

Provided that the therapist is calibrating all the time and noticing sensory feedback, he will recognise when the client has taken on the new belief. If the client stays quiet and appears to be processing internally, it is appropriate (after pausing for a short while) to ask what it is he is thinking. This will enable you to ensure that he is incorporating the new belief in the most useful way.

Often a client will find that once he has released the feelings associated with the original experience, he will gain insight into why subsequent events occurred in his life. This pattern can now stop.

22. *Follow-Up*

If a client were to undergo a subsequent GOLD Counselling analysis approximately three to four weeks after the original analysis had been worked through, it would be possible to determine whether other, previously-uncovered issues are now revealing themselves. We have always found that, provided the central belief core has been eliminated correctly, this follow-up map will always be structured significantly differently, with many of the old issues having just faded away and being no longer of any consequence whatsoever.

While this approach is very useful for a therapist undergoing his training so that he can recognise, first hand, how powerful the GOLD Counselling approach is at permanently removing limiting beliefs, we would not recommend carrying this out with a client unless he specifically requested a follow-up session. You should not need to prove that this technique works; it should be sufficient for you to know you are right and that the technique does work. After all, the change is natural and will come, whether the client notices it or not.

Section Three:

GOLD Counselling Case Studies

Introduction to Section Three

Section Three contains a selection of examples showing how GOLD Counselling has been used to facilitate change in clients. As you work through the examples you will notice that the complexity increases. You will find that, in some cases, additional topics have had to be prepared before the presenting problems could be worked through. In every case, however, the same approach, the same language and the same technique has been applied.

23. Case Studies

23.1 Overview of case studies

Let us suppose that your client has produced a list under the topic heading of **"I am"**. When asked to go back to locate the primary belief, the client speaks of the time when he had been falsely accused of stealing money and had received a reprimand from his mother. A way of questioning your client from this position would be:

"Where did you first learn to believe that you are guilty?"

On consideration of this question the client identified that the money had been given to him by his grandmother. From this position you would encourage your client to discover who should have accepted the label of being guilty in that situation. Your next question could be:

"So what I am hearing you say is that it was your mother who was guilty of accusing you falsely?"

Let your client focus his mind on this question. This allows the client time to gain the understanding that this question is inferring. Once the client has accepted the question and answered it positively, you should reinforce and augment the belief by asking the client to repeat with his internal voice statements such as:

"I believe my mother should feel guilty for making a false accusation."

or

"I believe my mother is guilty of falsely accusing me."

Once the client has resolved this individual learning about being guilty, it would be appropriate to identify whether there are additional experiences in his life coded as being guilty.

In order to ascertain where he may be, the client could now ask himself:

"... and where else did I learn to believe that I am guilty?"

As you review the case studies, we recommend that you construct a belief map for each one. In this way, you will be able to follow more closely the approach used by the therapist to facilitate change in the client.

23.2 Exam nerves case study

In this case study a client presented himself for treatment to help reduce or eliminate examination nerves.

Topic: *Exam Nerves*

A   I get it wrong

B   I can't focus

C   I know I'm a good student

D   I'm interested in the subject

E   I get nervous

F   People stare

G   I study hard

H   I have to get it right

I   People depend on me getting it right

J   I feel stupid

K   Confusing

L   I know the answers

Once the client had created the above list, he was asked to link the items and the result was as follows:

A   I get it wrong   L

B   I can't focus   C

C   I know I'm a good student   K

D   I'm interested in the subject   G

E   I get nervous   A

F   People stare   A

G   I study hard   D

H   I have to get it right   E

I   People depend on me getting it right   A

J   I feel stupid   A

K   Confusing   L

L   I know the answers   J

If you review this list you will notice from the collection of thoughts about the topic of examinations that the client has certain opposing beliefs. This is not unusual and would be expected, as indicated by the pre-supposi-tions of GOLD Counselling (refer back to Chapter 10 for further clarifica-tion).

We are not asking him to justify why he thinks what he thinks. We have no need for comments such as "*…and I feel stupid because I know I should be able to get it right.*" All that is required is a list of his thoughts about the selected topic.

From the previous list of thoughts the client had written, the items have been linked together as set out below. You will notice that there are two sets of beliefs which are functioning in order to support this topic. These are held in place by two separate primary belief structures, **A-L-J** and **D-G**. Of these, the first structure is the one containing the negative beliefs and if you look at the number of supporting secondary beliefs around this structure, you will recognise that most of the client's energy will be expended in supporting beliefs **A** then **L**.

A	**I get it wrong**	**L**
B	I can't focus	C
C	I know I'm a good student	K
D	**I'm interested in the subject**	**G**
E	I get nervous	A
F	People stare	A
G	**I study hard**	**D**
H	I have to get it right	E
I	People depend on me getting it right	A
J	**I feel stupid**	**A**
K	Confusing	L
L	**I know the answers**	**J**

This can be expressed using the GOLD Counselling mapping technique in a pictorial format.

Exams Nerves

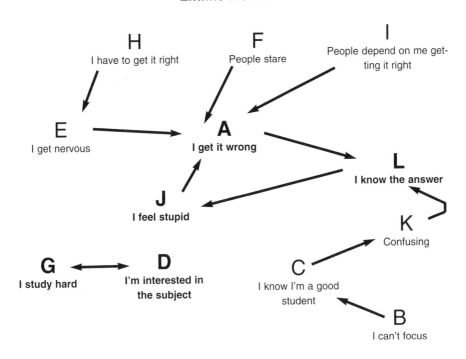

Once we have this framework we then move on to ask the client about his belief in a very precise and specific way.

Therapist: *So you believe that you get it wrong?*

Client: *Yes.*

Therapist: *As you relax there... your conscious mind still and quiet... you may take some time now... remembering that we spoke about... learning... how we learn to believe; and that you could, right now... take the time necessary to help yourself discover something about... your beliefs. Perhaps it is something that your unconscious mind... can shed some light on... a particular belief... and I know that your unconscious mind is always proud of its ability to fulfil your beliefs. Proud of its ability to show you all the necessary information ... including where you first learned that belief... "Exam Nerves, I get it wrong." That's right... just hold that thought in your mind... Just think "Where did I learn to believe that I believe Exam Nerves, I get it wrong?" and wait... and in a moment your unconscious mind will show you where it first learned to believe "Exam Nerves, I get it wrong."*

The client then found himself remembering a particular time when he was in a classroom at school. There was a competition in which the class had been divided into two groups. The teacher was playing a type of quiz game and the students were required to answer a general question. The client remembered that one particular question was asked and no-one on the client's side knew the answer. The teacher had put pressure on the client to answer the question and so finally, under pressure, he gave an answer that someone else had shouted out before... and it was wrong.

Getting this wrong cost his team the game and because of this he was abused and made to feel terrible by the other students. The client remembered feeling stupid, and then how the others were saying things like *"You always get it wrong."* The ironic thing about all this was that the client had indeed known the correct answer.

However, the problem seemed to stem from the fact that, at that moment, the client was so humiliated that things were never the same again. His classmates continued to tease him for much of the remainder of the term.

The flow of questioning at this point proceeded as follows:

Therapist: *If I heard you right, you believe that you get it wrong?*

Client: *Yes.*

Therapist: *So what you mean is that on that day, at that time, in that class-room, with that question?*

Client: *Yes.*

Therapist: *So there are other times when you got it right in a test?*

Client: *(A slower, deeper, considered answer) Yes.*

Therapist: *So when you look back to that time in the classroom then... you got it wrong then?*

Client: *Yes.*

Therapist: *So what do you mean about you **always** get it wrong?*

Client: *Well, I don't always get it wrong.*

Therapist: *So what is it that you believe?*

Client: *I see... well I believe that sometimes I get it wrong and sometimes I get it right.*

From this position the therapy continued dealing with other issues, this one having been resolved.

23.3 Public speaking case study

The client was a twenty-six-year-old male lawyer who was in his final year at law school when attending our practice. He had a serious problem with public speaking and with his self-esteem. This affected him so much that although he was deaf in one ear he would not wear a hearing aid for fear of people noticing this and laughing at him.

Topic: *Public speaking*

A	**Everyone should be able to do it without worry**	**B**
B	**I can't do it, obviously**	**A**
C	Public speaking does not have to be serious	D
D	If you make a mess of it, it's not a question of life or death	E
E	But I feel for me it is a question of life or death	B
F	Public speaking is something that should be enjoyed	G
G	I personally hate it enormously	E
H	**Public speaking should be used to advance a person's career**	**I**
I	**My career will go backwards if I can't master it**	**H**
J	Public speaking is an opportunity to express one's views or feelings	H
K	Public speaking should not frighten a person	A
L	I feel stupid	K
M	Public speaking should not give a person sleepless nights	K
N	But I get sleepless nights before my speeches	M

O   Good public speakers can make a lot of money by persuasion through their arguments   H

P   Public speech should make the audience listen   O

Q   I feel I bore them   P

Within this belief map there was found to be two sets of primary beliefs, **A-B** and **H-I** as set out in the belief map.

Public Speaking

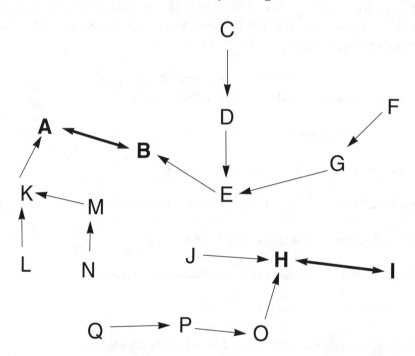

A	Everyone should be able to do it without worry	B
B	I can't do it, obviously	A
C	Public speaking does not have to be serious	D
D	If you make a mess of it, it's not a question of life or death	E
E	But I feel for me it is a question of life or death	B
F	Public speaking is something that should be enjoyed	G
G	I personally hate it enormously	E
H	**Public speaking should be used to advance a person's career**	I
I	**My career will go backwards if I can't master it**	H

J	Public speaking is an opportunity to express one's views or feelings	H
K	Public speaking should not frighten a person	A
L	I feel stupid	K
M	Public speaking should not give a person sleepless nights	K
N	But I get sleepless nights before my speeches	M
O	Good public speakers can make a lot of money by persuasion through their arguments	H
P	Public speech should make the audience listen	O
Q	I feel I bore them	P

Once this had been ascertained, we asked our client to relax and make himself comfortable so that he could begin focusing on his unconscious mind. The questioning then took the following path:

Therapist:	*…and ask yourself, where did I learn to believe the belief Public Speaking, I can't do it, obviously?*

Client: *My Dad.*

Therapist: *Tell me about it.*

Client: *I'm four years old and in the front room trying to build a Lego wall. Dad is there. He keeps saying "You can't do it. I'm telling you, you can't do it." I go to the kitchen to ask my mother to help me but she is too busy. She is cooking and looking after my baby sister. She says "Ask your father to help you." But I know he will just say, "I told you, you can't do it".*

Therapist: *So, your father believed then that you could not build that Lego wall. Is that right?*

Client: *I don't know. It was his way of challenging us to make us do better. He thought that if he challenged us we would try even harder and then be able to do things.*

Therapist: *But it didn't work that time, did it?*

Client: *No. It made me believe that I could not do it.*

Therapist: *So am I right in saying that your father gave you this mistaken belief?*

Client: *Yes, but he did not do it to harm me.*

Therapist: *That's right. But it did harm you. Don't you think it's time you gave that belief back to where and who it came from, back to your father?*

Client: *Yes.*

The next steps in the session consisted of our client's visualisation of that scene once again, but this time he saw himself wearing a sash that was much too big and baggy for him with the wording "I can't do it" on it. He then visualised putting the sash around his father whom it fitted perfectly.

Therapist: How does that feel?

Client: It feels good. I know that I can do it, I can do anything I try to do, I guess I've always known that really but there was a part of me that believed differently.

Therapist: And now?

Client: Now I know I can – that the belief is gone.

An interesting post-script to this GOLD Counselling analysis was that the client and his partner turned up at our practice four months later. He had passed his final examinations and had received a good job offer. A major part of the examination was a presentation to the lecturer, the class and external examiners in which he was required to argue a case which he had been assigned.

23.4 Weight control case study

Barbara was a fifty-year-old nurse who had been battling with weight problems for years, ever since her divorce at twenty-six from an abusive policeman. She remarried at twenty-nine and seemed very happy. She told us she loved crusty white bread and that this was her biggest downfall.

Topic: *Food*

A	I enjoy food	C
B	Food is healthy	C
C	Food makes me fat	E
D	**Eating food can comfort**	E
E	**When I see food I have to eat it**	D
F	Food can kill	A
G	I enjoy feeding other people	B

Within this belief structure, the primary beliefs were focused at the connections of **D-E.**

Food

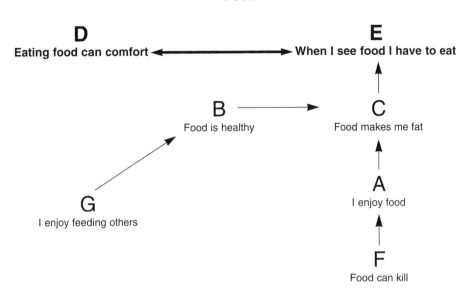

We then asked Barbara to close her eyes and relax using a very simple breathing exercise.

Therapist: *Where did I learn to believe the belief that when I see food I have to eat it?*

Client: *I don't know. I can see a man's face. I know him but I'm not sure who he is.*

Therapist: *Allow yourself to drift backwards in time until you recognise the man.*

Client: *I don't know, I just know I know him.*

Therapist: *You may have to go way back, perhaps to your early childhood even to find him.*

Client: *He's a friend of my brother's. God. I haven't seen him in years.*

Therapist: *Tell me, when did you first meet your brother's friend?*

Client: *They were at school together. I remember him having dinner with us at Gran's.*

Therapist: Tell me about dinner at Gran's.

Client: (Pause, now with tears rolling down her face) The whole family was always there for Sunday dinner and many times our friends were there as well. We used to eat in the kitchen. Gran had a really big old oak table and we would all sit down at the table. It was really nice, we'd talk about all sorts of things and the atmosphere was always lovely in Gran's kitchen. I remember there was always a basket of crusty rolls in the middle of the table, whenever we went there. Sometimes us children would go there during the week and Gran would look after us. She was always cooking or baking so we were usually in the kitchen.

Therapist: Imagine yourself there in that kitchen now and tell me how it feels.

Client: It's really nice and comfortable and it feels safe. Gran was always there if we wanted her.

Therapist: Describe the kitchen.

Barbara proceeded to do so in great detail including the basket of crusty rolls that was always on the table and Gran making the children rolls whenever they felt hungry or needed cheering up. She still had tears pouring down her face while explaining this.

Therapist: So what do those crusty bread rolls mean to you?

Client: Comfort and security.

The next step in the GOLD Counselling analysis session was to carry out repair work with Barbara. She visualised the kitchen with a vase of flowers on the table replacing the bread rolls. Barbara has since lost about two stone and has joined a health and fitness club where she is doing very well.

23.5 Arachnophobia case study

This woman was in her thirties. When asked how long she had been a phobic, she replied that it was as long as she could remember, so the topic chosen was **"Spiders"**.

Topic: *Spiders*

A	Hairy	M
B	Dark	N
C	Big	F
D	Ugly	T
E	Fat	A
F	Beastly	G
G	Scary	H
H	Frightening	P
I	Sick in stomach	T
J	Scream	W
K	Shaky	O
L	**Spooky**	**V**
M	Creepy	V
N	Dark corners	V
O	Twitchy/nervous/edgy	W
P	**Fast**	**W**
Q	Threatening	G
R	**Pathetic**	**Y**

S   Non-threatening   Y

T   Revolting   M

U   Spasmo   J

V   Lurking   **L**

W   Surprise   **P**

X   Pretty (small ones)   S

Y   Sad little creatures   **R**

Z   Hideous   I

AA Extreme revulsion   Z

AB Shock/fright   J

AC Relief (when dead) but then again there's always another one
      somewhere   Z

As discussed previously, some beliefs which are identified will be useful and, as a therapist, you should act to keep these active. The primary belief structure **R-Y** is just such an example. In consequence, work was focused on the structure **P-W**, and specifically **"Fast"**.

Spiders

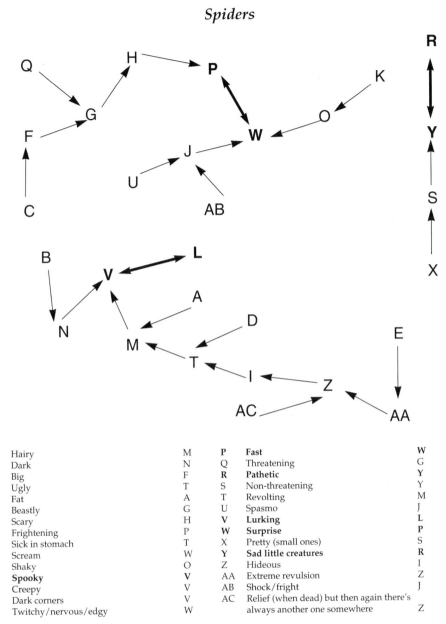

A	Hairy	M	**P**	**Fast**	W
B	Dark	N	Q	Threatening	G
C	Big	F	**R**	**Pathetic**	Y
D	Ugly	T	S	Non-threatening	Y
E	Fat	A	T	Revolting	M
F	Beastly	G	U	Spasmo	J
G	Scary	H	**V**	**Lurking**	L
H	Frightening	P	**W**	**Surprise**	P
I	Sick in stomach	T	X	Pretty (small ones)	S
J	Scream	W	**Y**	**Sad little creatures**	R
K	Shaky	O	Z	Hideous	I
L	**Spooky**	V	AA	Extreme revulsion	Z
M	Creepy	V	AB	Shock/fright	J
N	Dark corners	V	AC	Relief (when dead) but then again there's	
O	Twitchy/nervous/edgy	W		always another one somewhere	Z

The client was then asked the question *"Where did I learn to believe the belief spider is fast?"*. This question was repeated and repeated and from this her unconscious mind led her to remembering being on the toilet next to the sink. Next she recollected seeing a spider appear from the sink and immediately abreacted with a scream. We then replayed the original scene to its conclusion and she was then able to see that the spider had been frightened itself and had run away.

When she returned for her next visit and was asked about spiders she replied, *"Well to be honest, I haven't noticed any"*.

23.6 Self-sabotage case study

This client had a problem with generating more income and felt he never had enough money.

Topic: Money

A	It is difficult to get in large amounts	C
B	It is energy	C
C	Absolute belief will manifest any amount	D
D	**Money is unspiritual**	**F**
E	Having achieved a fortune leaves a career vacuum	B
F	**Having a fortune may cut me off from any further necessary development**	**D**
G	Can be dangerous in large amounts (personal attack, etc.) *	
H	Can provide opportunities to explore personal development *	
I	Can provide the means to spread the word *	

Money

This brief list revealed the primary belief structure of **D – F**. Working on the belief *"Money is unspiritual"* took the client back to being in a classroom in Australia when he was twelve. He remembered hearing his scripture teacher saying *"It is harder for a rich man to enter the kingdom of heaven than for a camel to pass through the eye of a needle"*. The client observed that although the teacher believed she was right, she was, in fact, in error. The client knew that many rich men do wonderful works with their money; work that would be impossible without it. The client was then able to revise this incorrect and limiting belief to *"Money is a spiritual neutral"*.

In addition the belief *"Having a fortune leaves a career vacuum"* has now been changed to *"Having achieved a fortune will help me expand my personal development."*

* The last three beliefs were not included in the analysis map. These were used to develop a separate map, unrelated to this case study. However, this list shows how one topic will often reveal other relevant information which will need to be treated separately (see Chapter 13.2 for further information).

23.7 Anger case study

Stuart is a forty-two-year-old management consultant. During the course of his sessions it had become apparent that he had suppressed a lot of anger.

Topic: *Anger*

A	Pure	B
B	I have a right to be angry	G
C	**You have no right to trample on me**	D
D	**I have rights**	G
E	Why can't things be perfect	L
F	Recognise I'm OK	G
G	**I matter**	C
H	You have no right to try to hurt me	K
I	I do not hurt people	H
J	Get things done	K
K	How dare you	C
L	I expect to be treated as an equal	C

Anger

The theme within Stuart's list was of anger focused at one person. The primary belief structure of **C-D-G** bore this out. In addition, three specific issues kept on appearing during previous sessions:

- Being stuck

- Getting to the edge and then drawing back

- Anger at his father for allowing his grandmother to dominate the family

When he went back in his mind to his childhood he would easily slip into third position, adopt an observatory role and repeat verbatim what was being said to him. His memories were infused with a strong symbolic content.

Therapist: *Focus on that angry feeling, really feel that anger... intensify it. Think about HOW DARE YOU! (feeding back his exact words to describe the feeling). Now tell me where did I learn to believe the belief I have been trampled on, that someone has tried to hurt me?*

Client: *She's very angry with me now. I'm telling you after all she's done for me, ungrateful, she's fuming, like a dragon breathing fire, like a witch going to do things to me. Mum's crying, she's frightened, doesn't want any harm to come to me, begging my Gran not to hurt me. "Please don't, Mum, leave him alone." I'm not afraid. God she's going crazy, like a malevolent devil, she's so angry. How dare I? Revenge, she's going to have revenge, scary. My Dad's just looking over, he's not taking any part at all. Mum's so upset. I'm calm, don't dislike her, need to know, understand why she did it. God she's angry.*

Therapist: *Why she did what, Stuart?*

Client: *Malicious, horrible to my Dad. I can see her now a frail old lady. Very bitter about her husband being taken from her, alone. My dad, it's not his fault. She's so spiteful in her anger. I'm running around like an animal being chained to something, trying to get away, screaming, scared she's going to get me back for this, for talking about it now, after all she's done, taking my Dad in when he had no home.*

His comments continued in this way for a further ten minutes. Then we passed Stuart our punch pillow and we spent the remainder of the session facilitating in him the release of the anger he had held onto. After the session he said that before then he had never remembered his Gran becoming angry like that and that while in the session he was afraid that she was going to take her revenge on him for speaking out. She had actually died when he was twelve.

Once this release had occurred, Stuart was able to understand where his trait of *"getting to the edge and then backing away"* had come from. At our next session he was much calmer and more relaxed.

23.8 Me case study

While there are various specific GOLD Counselling topics which we have identified as appropriate for use with clients, a standard topic we use with clients is "Me", This can be used to reveal issues relating to poor self-image or similar limitations. We would not apply this at the first session, but possibly by session three. This case study which follows was focused on this heading.

Kioto is a Japanese woman aged forty-five. She works as a PA to the director of a large Japanese company, one that is very tradition-bound. Kioto was an only child brought up by her parents in Japan, then when she was in her mid-twenties she came to England. Her father was a dentist, a gambler, a drug-addict and an alcoholic. Her mother committed the cardinal sin of taking a lover who followed the family every time they were forced to move by her father's behaviour at work. The family set success by academic achievement, particularly scientific. However, Kioto is creative rather than scientifically-oriented.

Topic: *Me*

A	I was not loved by my parents	**B**
B	I lack a good model of a happy life	**C**
C	I could have achieved more if my childhood was not hampered by family problems	**A**
D	I don't know how to love unconditionally	L
E	I'm more flirtatious than I want others to think	L
F	I have to work really hard to make a living	**G**
G	My life will always be hard	**F**
H	I'm very materialistic	**L**
I	I'm fairly snobbish	**R**
J	I am artistic	U
K	I am stingy but I pretend not to be	H
L	I am selfish but this seems to be the only way to survive	**H**
M	I am a victim of circumstances	A
N	There is a part of me that has not grown properly	A
O	I cannot be relied on	L
P	If I finally conclude that my life will not work out, then I can kill myself	B
Q	My enemy is myself	P
R	I need to keep a good appearance and not to show my real self to the outside	**I**
S	I need to be very conscious of what others will think of me	I
T	There is a new me which is struggling to come out	A
U	I am stubborn	L

Me

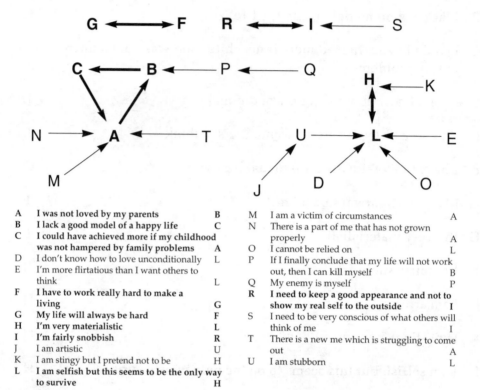

A	I was not loved by my parents	B	M	I am a victim of circumstances		A
B	I lack a good model of a happy life	C	N	There is a part of me that has not grown		
C	I could have achieved more if my childhood			properly		A
	was not hampered by family problems	A	O	I cannot be relied on		L
D	I don't know how to love unconditionally	L	P	If I finally conclude that my life will not work		
E	I'm more flirtatious than I want others to			out, then I can kill myself		B
	think	L	Q	My enemy is myself		P
F	I have to work really hard to make a		R	I need to keep a good appearance and not to		
	living	G		show my real self to the outside		I
G	My life will always be hard	F	S	I need to be very conscious of what others will		
H	I'm very materialistic	L		think of me		I
I	I'm fairly snobbish	R	T	There is a new me which is struggling to come		
J	I am artistic	U		out		A
K	I am stingy but I pretend not to be	H	U	I am stubborn		L
L	I am selfish but this seems to be the only way					
	to survive	H				

This list was structured around the following primary beliefs: C – A – B, G – F, H – L and I – R. Having reviewed the list, we asked Kioto to focus on a specific question and the following then occurred:

Therapist: Where did I first learn to believe the belief I am selfish?

Client: I caused my father to lose face in front of visitors.

Therapist: Tell me about it.

Client: I was little, only about maybe two or three, and I was, I don't know, making a noise or trying to get his attention or something and my father had to shout at me in front of his visitors. After, when they were gone, he told me what a bad girl I was, how I made him lose face.

Therapist: So where did I learn to believe that I believe I am selfish?

Client: *Well, I taught myself, because if I was being bad and causing my father to lose face, then I thought to myself I must be selfish.*

Therapist: *So do you believe a little child of two or three wanting her father's attention or making a bit of noise is being selfish?*

Client: *No, that is just natural behaviour that I was being forced to suppress.*

Therapist: *So do you now believe that you are selfish?*

Client: *I must be because I manipulate people.*

Therapist: *So where did I learn to believe that I believe that I manipulate people?*

Client: *At school. Excellence at school, especially in the sciences, was what my parents appreciated, so I studied and worked really hard, all those hours. I worked to make them appreciate me. I knew if I could get good marks and be top of the class they would love me. But even though I worked very hard, I never came higher than second.*

Therapist: *So by working very hard to try to get your parents' love, you were manipulating them, is that right?*

Client: *I've got to open my eyes, I feel so dizzy, I feel sick.*

Therapist: *Kioto, that is your resistance talking, are you ready to work through that to get to the information we need right now to help you?*

Client: *Yes, yes, yes, I was manipulating them to get their love.*

Therapist: *So that every child who works hard to gain her parents' approval is selfish and manipulative?*

Client: *Well, no, not really. But, I was.*

Therapist: *Children are born with the right to unconditional love. Their parents have a duty to love and cherish and nurture the child. Tell me, who is failing, who is being selfish when a child has to work and manipulate to get attention, never mind the love that is her right?*

There was silence from Kioto and a few tears.

Therapist: Kioto, it's not your fault.

The flood gates then opened and she was almost howling like an animal, repeatedly saying "*It's not my fault*". After a minute of sobs and tears the session continued.

Therapist: So do you believe that you are selfish and manipulate people?

Client: No! It really was not my fault, they were selfish, not me. Expecting so much from me but never giving me any respect, any love.

Therapist: If that mistaken selfish belief had a physical form what would it be?

Client: It wears a metal suit, like iron and it has a long spiky nose.

Therapist: What would be needed to destroy that mistaken belief forever?

Client: A big hammer; then I can hit it over the head – BANG – and flatten it and completely destroy it. (At this point Kioto was carrying out the actions of swinging a heavy hammer over her head then crashing it down on to her lap, laughing and crying at the same time, bouncing around in the chair.) It is done.

It is interesting to observe that we have invariably found that when a topic is being dealt with that has a strong degree of emotional content, particularly where there is a strong element of denial linked to it, a physical form of resistance will manifest itself, attempting to disrupt the proceedings. The dizziness as experienced by Kioto is an example of this.

23.9 Control case study

Gemma is a thirty-four-year-old director of a small manufacturing company. She initially consulted us for problems with panic attacks which she was experiencing in a variety of situations. These had expanded to include signing cheques in front of others, standing in queues, pouring coffee for visitors, driving (she was no longer driving), being in trains or aeroplanes, being around strangers – in particular those in positions of power or authority.

Gemma was terrified of losing control and did not want to enter any altered states. It was her dislike of the idea of hypnosis which meant she was willing to consider using GOLD Counselling to alleviate her problem.

This fear was so profound that she would not even sit in an inclined chair but instead always sat on a hard high-backed chair.

However, she was incredibly imaginative and was very capable at recall. Her first panic attack had occurred three years ago when she was asked to serve coffee to visitors – she had started to shake so badly that she had to get someone else in to make and distribute the coffees.

Gemma has a very abusive mother and an ineffectual father. The issue of control had repeatedly come up in earlier sessions so she was asked to complete a GOLD Counselling list on the topic of **"Control"**.

Topic: *Control*

A	**Shaking, non-controllable**	F
B	Not obeying, not assertive (work)	C
C	**Bullying by my family**	E
D	Passenger (car)	E
E	**Anger**	C
F	**Foolish**	A
G	Training (on the job)	E
H	Travel (train, aeroplane)	F
I	Loss of control – vertigo	E
J	Ian, America. His sister	C

Control

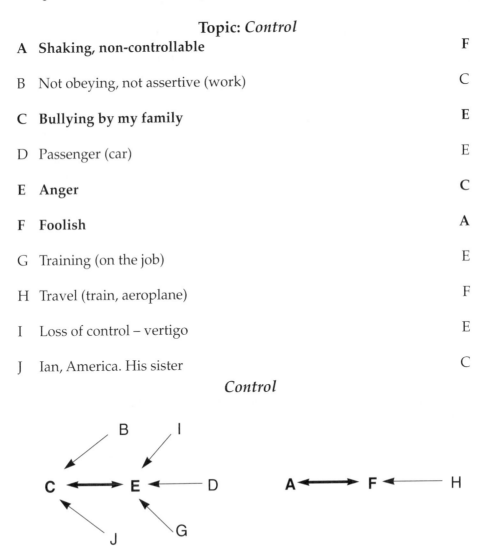

It can be seen that the primary belief structures were **A – F** and **C – E.**

Item J relates to Gemma's husband, Ian. He had been in America for a while where his sister lives. She had arranged a piece of work for him and was pressurising them both to move to America as she felt that Ian's work prospects would be enhanced there. Ian's sister apparently had a personality similar to Gemma's mother, one which is domineering and verbally abusive.

Because of her fears of losing control, the session was commenced by just asking her to close her eyes and to let her conscious mind be receptive to whatever was to drift up from her unconscious.

Therapist: Where did I learn to believe the belief I am foolish?

Client: I feel foolish when I start shaking and then I get very angry at myself, my lack of assertiveness and knowing that I'm not in control.

From this point, she digressed into explaining various incidents. Firstly that she had been bullied by her mother and brother. Then that her sister-in-law was trying to convince Ian to move to America when she did not want to give up her job and go there, and that she certainly did not want to live near this woman. Then that her mother had repeatedly told her that she "had nearly ripped my guts out being born", and lastly about all the things that she was annoyed with herself about. The final digression was of a memory of her father bringing strangers to the house one day who were dressed very similarly to the visitors at work at the time of her panic attack. Apparently Gemma had been about six at the time that her father brought those "men in suits" home.

Therapist: So where did I learn to believe that I believe that I am not in control?

Client: It is something to do with those visitors of Dad's, they were important to him, to his business.

After a great deal of exploration, and we were getting nowhere fast, we felt it was necessary to ask Gemma what had happened earlier in the day, before her father had brought his guests home.

Client: We'd been up to London on the train, I'm not sure but I think my Gran was there as well. The tube was packed with football supporters, there was nowhere to sit and they were all so big. Someone gave Gran a seat but Mum and me were standing in the middle. They were all shouting and singing and then they started swaying, pushing from one end of the carriage to the other. I was hanging on to Mum and we couldn't do anything, we had to move with them. They were all so big and I couldn't stop shaking. I was *getting squashed and I could hardly breathe and I was frightened I would fall and they would trample on me but they wouldn't stop. A man lifted me up over their heads and pushed me over to Gran and I was screaming and trying to hold on to Mum but she couldn't move, she was stuck in the middle and we couldn't get off because the carriage was so full. We had to stay on until they all got off and we missed our stop. I was so frightened I thought we were all going to die. Mum and Gran were trying not to show they were frightened but they were and I knew they were and that made me even more scared.*

All the time Gemma was speaking she was crying and shaking. Afterwards, she opened her eyes and said she now realised that this was where it came from. The following week she told us she had started driving again and served coffee without shaking at work (although she had been worried about this all day until the visitors arrived) but was still nervous about shopping and queues. Gemma had always gone shopping late at night when there would not be many people around and had always prepared the cheque prior to leaving the house. Her alcohol consumption had also dropped sharply during the week. She said she was feeling far more confident and in control than she had for years.

During a later session Gemma was taken through a list she had prepared on **"Queues"** and found that her limiting belief was about holding people up. Using the GOLD Counselling technique we arrived at a memory of how Dad had a thing about not being late or holding people up and used to get very angry with her if she was late in the mornings when he was taking her to school. He would deliver lectures about holding people up and how she was not important enough to keep people waiting.

The following week she came in almost dancing. That week she had been able to visit a major department store (previously a problem since she was required to pay on her charge card), gone on the lifts and escalators (previously impossible because of a fear of holding people up) and finished the day by buying petrol without a pre-signed cheque. All of this had taken place without any problems whatsoever.

At work there had been a group of important clients visiting. Gaining their contract could mean the difference between the company staying in business or folding. She had been a bit nervous for approximately ten minutes prior to their arrival. Also, she had been able to speak to her Managing Director about her always having to make the coffee because she was a woman. This had been bothering her for a long time but she had been too frightened to say anything.

23.10 Depression case study

This client had been suffering from recurring bouts of severe depression. The client was a woman of twenty-seven, married, with no children. Before working on "Depression," a map on "Anger" was prepared.

Topic: *Anger*

A	Red	E
B	Crying	D
C	Feeling let down	K
D	Tears	B
E	Violence	A
F	Shouting	R
G	Loud	H
H	Won't listen	E
I	Unfair	G
J	Hate	N
K	Helpless	L
L	Impenetrable	H
M	Frightening	P
N	Wanting to hit out	R
O	Wanting to hurt	P
P	No control	N
Q	Feeling sick	R
R	Shaking	E

Anger

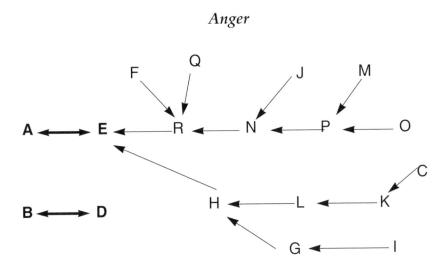

The GOLD Counselling list is structured around the primary beliefs **A-E** and **B-D.** The decision was taken to work on **"Violence"** and the session went as follows.

Therapist: *Where did I learn to believe the belief anger, violence? How did I learn to believe the belief anger, violence?*

The client found herself taken back to a childhood memory of violence between her parents. She was sitting on the stairs, seeing and hearing a violent argument. She can see her parents through a doorway. She was frightened just sitting there alone on the stairs. Their voices were loud, she felt their anger and she feels helpless. She didn't know where her brother was and felt totally helpless.

The adult client was then asked to imagine in her mind's eye going into the scene and rescuing the child. The adult took the child and stepped onto a cloud. The cloud floated up into a warm, blue, sunny sky. The adult hugged the child and told the child that she is safe and loved. The adult then told the child that anger was violence, back then, back there, in that scene between mother and father – now you can believe that you are safe, secure and loved.

Four days after this, a recurring bad dream that the client had been having about her brother, in which she felt anger towards him, stopped.

The client was then asked to prepare a list on **"Depression."**

Topic: *Depression*

A	Black	B
B	Dark	E
C	Despair	F
D	Guilt	N
E	**Hide**	V
F	Hopelessness	N
G	Worthless	O
H	**Weary**	S
I	Drowning	R
J	Lethargic	S
K	Confusion	R
L	Endless	N
M	**Blank**	**Q**
N	No control	P
O	Pathetic	U
P	Frustrated	K
Q	**Dazed**	**M**
R	Frightened	T
S	**Exhausted/weak**	**H**
T	Miserable	V
U	Tearful/emotional	T

V Shutting self off from outside world   E

W   Avoid conflicts/questions   E

Depression

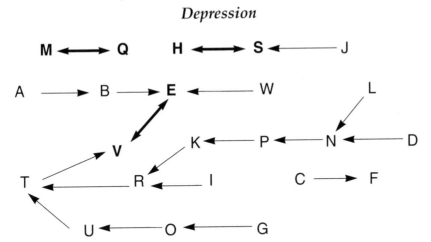

It was decided that we would work with **"Shutting self off from the outside world."**

Therapist: *Where did I learn to believe the belief depression, shutting self off from the outside world?*

Client: *I don't know.*

After a pause the procedure continued.

Therapist: *How did I learn to believe the belief depression, shutting self off from the outside world?*

Client: *I don't know.*

After a pause the procedure continued.

Therapist: *How did I learn to believe the belief depression, shutting self off from the outside world?*

Client: *I don't know.*

The client then recalled being a teenager and watching and listening to her parents arguing which then led to their fighting. She was distressed and left the family home and went to sit by the river. She had taken some pills with her. She was continually repeating, *"It's all my fault – I always get it wrong."*

Once she had arrived at the river she just sat there quietly thinking, feeling sadness and despair. She started to feel guilty about leaving her mother in the house and decided to return home.

She then remembered that her mother drinks and wanted to find a way of stopping her. She and her mother argued. Within the argument mother tells the client, *"It's all your fault"*, *"You take me for granted"* and *"I want to go away and leave you all to get on with it"*. The client felt that the situation was all her fault.

The client now focuses on the scene with her mother's drinking and feeling that it is all her fault that her mother drinks. The session then continued as follows:

Therapist: *Who can stop drinking?*

Client: *Mother.*

Therapist: *Who can change drinking?*

Client: *Mother.*

Therapist: *Who owns drinking?*

Client: *Mother.*

Therapist: *Whose drinking problem is this?*

Client: *Mother.*

Therapist: *Who can change it?*

Client: *Mother.*

The client was then asked *"What about me and how I feel?"*. The adult client, who is now feeling strong and confident, joins the client in the scene in her mind to explain to mother how she feels.

The adult client tells mother *"Drinking is your problem and you are the only one who can change it. It's not my fault"*. The confident client then takes the teenage client in her mind to a happy place where they feel safe. They have a hug and feel and know they are safe. They tell each other that Mum's problems are Mum's and that she owns them, both then and now, and that only Mum can deal with her own problems. The client then acknowledged that she is a caring and thoughtful person and can deal with and solve her own problems confidently.

Future-paced suggestions were then applied so that the client could carry out deep breathing exercises to feel relaxed and calm and to allow her to be able to deal with stressors in a relaxed, calm and confident manner. She was also guided to focus her attention on her breathing and find her calm place within herself whenever needed.

"Shutting self off from the outside world" occurred when the client escaped to the river to be alone. At the river the client felt *"Despair"* and considered taking her own life. She had felt that she had "No control" while watching her parents fighting. She had also felt *"Frustrated"*, *"Confused"* and *"Frightened"* while watching the scene. She had also felt *"Guilt"* about her mother's drinking problems.

The client was then asked to compile a list on "**Guilt**".

Topic: *Guilt*

A	Letting people down	B
B	Causing people problems	L
C	Causing people/family worries	L
D	**Not being there for other people**	**M**
E	Not doing anything	O
F	Worried	J
G	**Tense**	**I**
H	Feeling sick	J
I	**Restlessness**	**G**
J	**Frightened**	**L**
K	Avoiding contact with other people	O
L	**Feeling people will give up on me**	**N**

M Unreliable   **D**

N Unwanted   **L**

O Isolated   J

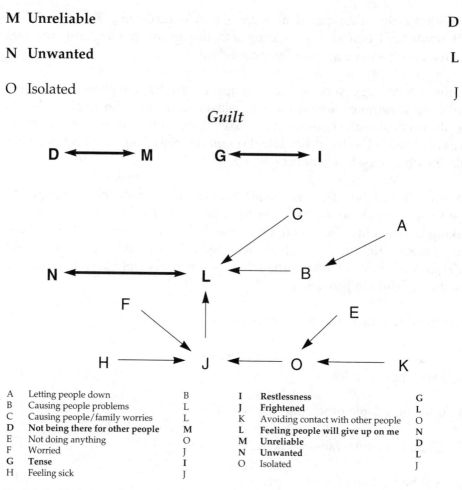

Guilt

A	Letting people down	B	I	Restlessness	G
B	Causing people problems	L	J	Frightened	L
C	Causing people/family worries	L	K	Avoiding contact with other people	O
D	**Not being there for other people**	M	L	**Feeling people will give up on me**	N
E	Not doing anything	O	M	Unreliable	D
F	Worried	J	N	Unwanted	L
G	**Tense**	I	O	Isolated	J
H	Feeling sick	J			

In this belief map there are three primary belief structures in operation, L-N, D-M and G-I.

Therapist: *Where did I learn to believe the belief guilt, people will give up on me?*

The client went back to her schooldays and to a time when she was bullied. She was in the changing room changing for gym. Two girls were picking on her. She recalls that she did not have any friends at school and was always alone. She was a good student, very quiet and shy and enjoyed learning but did not make friends. Her parents told her that she was just to ignore the other girls and get on with things. Nobody understood what she was going through.

In this memory she was feeling very frightened and wishing they would go away – they were taunting her. Seeing her start to release a tear down the side of her cheek prompts us to get her to cry and really let go, letting the tears really flow. The client then starts to cry and sob for the first time about this incident. Back then, she had always held on to her emotions and controlled herself in order to ensure that the bullies did not see her cry.

After letting the tears subside, the client was asked to imagine the person in that scene growing larger and larger as the girls came closer to her. As they taunt her, so she gets bigger and bigger. She was then asked to watch the girls' reactions. They became frightened of her and backed away.

Therapist: *Feel that power and strength within yourself now and look at them. Say to them all that you want to say, do to them all that you want to do.*

When she had finished she was then given the following guided suggestions. She was asked to imagine walking towards a door with a key in it.

Therapist: *Open the door and take the key with you. Step inside the room and lock the door. Be sure that the door is securely locked and that nobody can get in unless you choose to allow them. Turn round and notice that the room is warm and welcoming. It is filled with pink heart-shaped cushions. Go and sit down and get comfortable on the cushions. Feel warm and safe and know that this is a safe place for you to enter anytime you want to feel warmth, love, safety, security and peace. You can find this place in your mind anytime you choose.*

23.11 Relationships case study

The client was very anxious, nervous and totally lacking in self-esteem. He had sunk to an all-time low in his life. The first list on "**Relationships**" had confirmed what had already been discovered through other therapeutic interventions.

Topic: *Relationships*

A	Difficult	L
B	Hard	H
C	**Shouting**	M
D	**Fighting**	I
E	**Hate**	L
F	Hit	H
G	Busy	I
H	Sunday lunch	A
I	**Pain**	C
J	Love	E
K	Staying	B
L	**Mother**	D
M	**Unfair**	E

Relationships

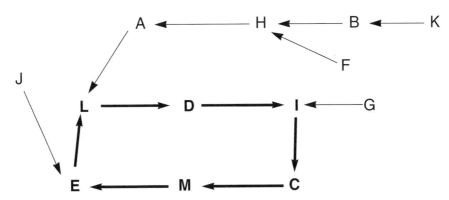

The primary belief structure for this client was **L – D – I – C – M – E**. Using this as a framework we worked with *"Mother", "Hate", "Sunday lunch"* and *"Unfair"*. It had been a shocking realisation to the client that he hated his mother for her unloving and critical attitude towards him all his life. Until coming into therapy he had believed that all parents had this attitude towards their children. The client also came to realise that his mother was incapable of loving anyone and not just himself. Also, after three failed marriages and a string of unhappy affairs the client had come to believe that relationships could be only hateful and unfair.

Through the work we did, the client came to understand where his beliefs on relationships were originally formed and, in fact, to whom those beliefs belonged. They were his mother's beliefs of how a relationship should be and not his own. The client also came to understand that our beliefs at an unconscious level will always fulfil themselves. Hence the importance of finding out where our beliefs were formed and by whom. Thus we have the opportunity to locate our beliefs and how they were formed and, where necessary, to change those beliefs by acknowledging to whom they truly belong.

While we do not usually suggest a follow-up list, in this case we were still working with the client and asked him to complete a second list on **"Relationships"** two weeks later.

Topic: *Relationships*

A Happy	H
B Strong	C
C Love	E
D Respect	G
E Joy	F
F Giving	H
G Sharing	E
H Caring	L
I Space	D
J Time	A
K Easy	C
L Flow	J

Relationships

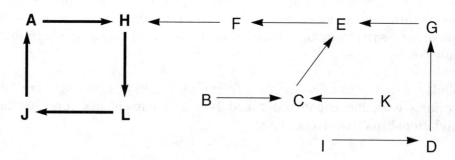

The fresh list revealed a primary belief structure of **A – H – L – J**. This is a significantly more liberating structure than previously.

23.12 Cancer case study

A woman client in her early forties is experiencing cancer for the third time. The first occurrence was over ten years ago, the second was four years ago and she is now undergoing chemotherapy for the third time. This woman originally came to discover ways of relaxing and reducing stress. Generally she had a poor self-image and was living in a very stressful environment. She is the mother of two children and presently the largest area of stress is being caused by not knowing if the cancer would recur.

Topic: *Cancer*

A	Scared	D
B	Guilt	C
C	Pain	P
D	Challenge	W
E	Panic	A
F	Helpless	L
G	Disbelief	S
H	Attention	V
I	Pity	P
J	Sad	P
K	Angry	V
L	Failure	R
M	Pressure	O
N	Change	W
O	Confused	N
P	Unfairness	G

Q Isolation   E

R Embarrassed   K

S Shocked   E

T Insecure   N

U Unattractive   I

V Negative   F

W Positive   P

Cancer

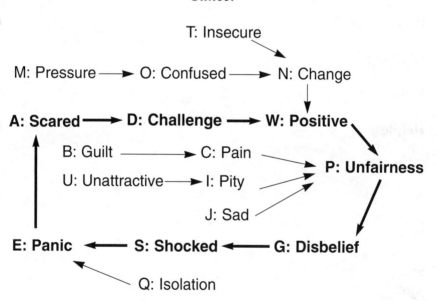

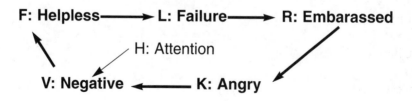

A	Scared	D		M	Pressure	O	
B	Guilt	C		N	Change	W	
C	Pain	P		O	Confused	N	
D	**Challenge**	W		P	**Unfairness**	G	
E	Panic	A		Q	Isolation	E	
F	Helpless	L		R	Embarrassed	K	
G	Disbelief	S		S	**Shocked**	E	
H	Attention	V		T	Insecure	N	
I	Pity	P		U	Unattractive	I	
J	Sad	P		V	**Negative**	F	
K	Angry	V		W	**Positive**	P	
L	Failure	R					

The point of weakness and the least anxiety-provoking item on the surface is **"Unfairness"**.

We had previously explained to the client, with some demonstrations, how beliefs are installed and also, at that time, she was taught how to relax her mind. We then asked the client the following question:

"Where did I learn to believe I believe cancer, unfairness?"

This question was repeated for about two minutes. The client then recalled that, at the age of approximately ten years, her Mother was on the telephone talking to her best friend's Mother saying how unfair it is and is consoling her best friend's Mother at the loss of her daughter who has died of leukaemia.

23.13 Eating disorders case study

This woman, was single, living with parents and her presenting problem was bulimia. From a previous list on the topic of **"I am"** a belief of **"Fat"** was extracted.

Topic: *Fat*

A	Ugly	GG
B	Huge	OO
C	Failure	T
D	**Mirror**	**RR**
E	**Uncomfortable**	**L**
F	Self-control	CC

G	Will-power	F
H	**Diet**	**I**
I	**Mum**	**H**
J	Sister	I
K	Stomach	L
L	**Bloated**	**E**
M	Nothing	MM
N	Thin	EE
O	Obsession	S
P	Attention	CC
Q	Ill	X
R	Worry	AA
S	**Constant**	**V**
T	**Food**	**W**
U	Disgraceful	JJ
V	**Always on my mind**	**S**
W	**Guilt**	**T**
X	Laxatives	N
Y	Sick	T
Z	**Panic**	**AA**
AA	**Weighing myself**	**Z**
BB	Scales	R

CC Achievement	**DD**
DD Proud	**CC**
EE Happier	**FF**
FF Feel good about myself	**EE**
GG Hate myself	QQ
HH Gross	OO
II Pig	JJ
JJ Compulsive eating	HH
KK Calories	T
LL Suffering	S
MM Lonely	LL
NN Bulges	PP
OO Rolls of fat	QQ
PP Hideous	OO
QQ Pinching fat	C
RR Always looking	**D**

Fat

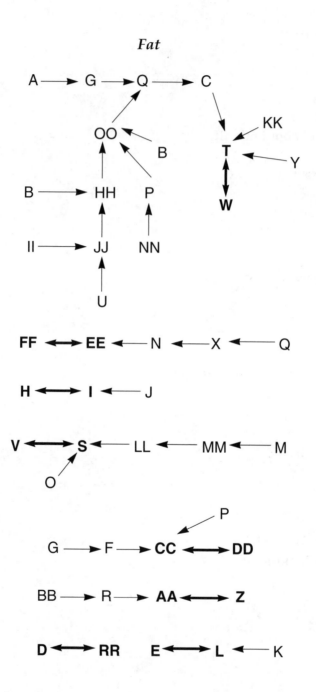

A	Ugly	GG		W	**Guilt**	**T**
B	Huge	OO		X	Laxatives	N
C	Failure	T		Y	Sick	T
D	**Mirror**	**RR**		Z	**Panic**	**AA**
E	Uncomfortable	L		AA	**Weighing myself**	**Z**
F	Self-control	CC		BB	Scales	R
G	Will-power	F		**CC**	**Achievement**	**DD**
H	**Diet**	**I**		**DD**	**Proud**	**CC**
I	**Mum**	**H**		**EE**	**Happier**	**FF**
J	Sister	I		**FF**	**Feel good about myself**	**EE**
K	Stomach	L		GG	Hate myself	QQ
L	**Bloated**	**E**		HH	Gross	OO
M	Nothing	MM		II	Pig	JJ
N	Thin	EE		JJ	Compulsive eating	HH
O	Obsession	S		KK	Calories	T
P	Attention	CC		LL	Suffering	S
Q	Ill	X		MM	Lonely	LL
R	Worry	AA		NN	Bulges	PP
S	**Constant**	**V**		**OO**	**Rolls of fat**	**QQ**
T	**Food**	**W**		PP	Hideous	OO
U	Disgraceful	JJ		QQ	Pinching fat	C
V	**Always on my mind**	**S**		**RR**	**Always looking**	**D**

We asked the client to repeat the following question:

"Where did I learn to believe that I believe Fat – Mum?".

The client finds herself looking at Mum looking at herself in the mirror. The child identifies with Mum and feels that she is going to be like her fat. Her stomach is hanging out with rolls of fat, and the client is sickened by this. She doesn't want to be like her – it's disgusting. The client feels *"Panic"* (Z) at the possibility. The client then feels *"Guilty"* (W) at having these thoughts about her own mother.

Client: *"How could I think such a thing about my mother? I hate myself for thinking it." "I am alone in my bedroom – it's always on my mind thinking that I will turn out to be like her. I get on the scales and panic."*

23.14 Learning difficulties case study

William is a very bright and active boy of twelve who is experiencing some difficulty with learning maths.

Topic: *Learning*

A	English teacher	F
B	English	A
C	**Maths**	**F**
D	Science	G
E	Hard	B
F	**Some is easy**	C
G	Learning easy	J
H	**Work**	**I**
I	**Enjoy**	**H**
J	Happy	K
K	As	M
L	**1s**	**M**
M	**Report**	L

Learning

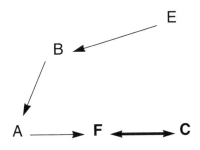

We decided to work with **"Learning is hard"**, because although the presenting problem was *"Maths"*, the words *"English"* and *"English teacher"* were listed as well and we felt that *"Hard"* would resolve the problem more quickly.

We asked William to repeat the question:

"Where did I learn to believe that I believe learning – hard?"

He recalled himself at the age of about seven years being sent to the headmistress' office because he had been naughty and written his name in a book. He didn't like her because she shouts. This headmistress teaches Maths and English and is telling William that *learning is the hardest thing he will ever have to do*.

Section Four:

How To Apply GOLD Counselling Techniques Within NLP Procedures

Introduction to Section Four

Within Section Four of this book we have developed the connections between GOLD Counselling and the techniques as incorporated within NLP. These connections are not meant to be exhaustive, and at our Counsellors' training workshops we would delve deeper into the full implications of the overlap. We feel, however, that for a competent therapist or practitioner it would be possible to quickly grasp the concepts documented herein and apply these ideas to your own practices. We have, therefore, briefly documented a suggested alternative approach for certain NLP techniques currently applied in therapeutic or training scenarios.

At the end of this section we have included a brief glossary of key words used within NLP. This is not meant to be an exhaustive list, it is purely to aid newcomers to NLP to understand some of the important terms within this field.

24. *How GOLD Counselling Integrates With NLP*

As you will have now discovered, the beliefs which we hold control every-thing we say, do and think. It is only by operating at this level – that of beliefs – that we can create permanent and deep change for our clients. Within NLP there have been created many techniques and these can be grouped into different types. One quite simple, yet by no means exhaus-tive, categorisation is to recognise that some techniques focus on language patterns, others focus on pseudo-orientation in time and others focus on pseudo-orientation in space. All these techniques have the capacity to create significant change for people.

However, unless the therapist can determine the underlying beliefs which explain why a client is carrying out his problem state or habit, change will not be permanent. By taking your client through a GOLD Counselling analysis it is possible to identify exactly what it is that is holding him back from achieving what he desires. Once this is released, the tools and techniques developed within NLP can then be used, knowing that the original barriers to success have been removed.

Within NLP there exists the concept of Meta-programs. (Dilts, R., 1990) These are the sensory filters which we use to sift and sort information and thoughts. When your client generates his list of beliefs you will be presented with a detailed audit of exactly what Meta-programs he applies to his thoughts. This will enable you to understand further how and why his current problems exist and then how to "speak his language" when helping him.

By asking your client to complete a list of beliefs for a chosen topic you will also be able to work with him using the appropriate modalities for the different elements of his problem. Since he has written down the thoughts in his own words, the exact language to be used has been presented to you.

As you read the next chapters you will recognise how the approach as set out within GOLD Counselling will enable you to become even more successful at using NLP by focusing your skills precisely on the correct areas of your client's experiences.

25. *Eliminating Operator Influence*

One of the paradigms within NLP is that you cannot not influence, you can only not notice the influence that you have made. When using GOLD Counselling this restriction no longer applies. You are now able to not influence the client since the information he provides will be in his own language and from his own mind. This is so for the following reasons:

- By asking him to develop a GOLD Counselling map on a subject of his own choice we have not influenced him.

- In asking the client to generate his own list of beliefs using his own language (including predicates and sub-modalities), we have not influenced him.

- By asking him to join the map together in a way that's right for him, we are again not influencing him.

- And, lastly, by asking that he take his mind back to a specific and central memory within his own belief map, we have not influenced him, only focused him.

This difference in the way GOLD Counselling works when compared to other therapeutic interventions is extremely important since if you are influencing your client, either by accident or design, it may well mean that when working with your client you will unconsciously guide him in the directions which *you* deem appropriate. In consequence, if his symptom or problem is related to something which you find uncomfortable to deal with, you may well not dig as deep into the true underlying reasons for the problem compared to other, more preferred subjects.

26. Anchoring: Why It So Often Isn't Permanent

26.1 Overview

Most of us have had times when we felt we were on top form, when everything just seemed to be going along perfectly. It was as if we just couldn't put a foot wrong. Conversely, there are also those days when whatever we do seems to go wrong. We say the wrong thing, do the wrong thing, or even forget to do things and end up feeling bad. Those positive states are often grouped together under the heading of good luck or good fortune, whereas when the negative states occur, many people put them down to having got out of the wrong side of the bed, or one of those types of days, or just one of those things.

In the same way, there are positive states which we can seem to achieve, often without thinking about them, such as falling in love or relaxing when lying back on a soft bed at the end of a long, hard day. Imagine the sounds of popping champagne corks and glasses tinkling together and most people would associate these sounds and images with joyful feelings.

The technical term for the way that one's body goes into these different states is through *anchoring*. An anchor can be simply and easily described as *any stimulus which evokes a consistent response pattern from a person* (Grinder & Bandler, 1981).

26.2 How anchors develop automatically

Anchors are all around us. We all develop anchors from a very early age. Consider how a baby learns that when he cries, his mummy will pick him up and comfort him, (or rather, he hopes that she will). These early anchors which are formed are automatic and many of the other anchors which we develop are formed in this automatic, unconscious way as well. Habits, such as learning to walk, riding a bike, or even understanding these words on the page in front of you now are examples of complex anchors. In each case, once learned they are consigned to the unconscious mind for it to administer and a very good job it does for us.

Problems arise as we grow up and we start to receive different and conflicting messages which have the effect of confusing us and reducing the clarity of our true feelings. Perhaps we have come from a background where we've only ever been praised for what we do, not who we are. Or perhaps we've been conditioned to get on and do things for ourselves and not to ask for help – even if we also feel that it's not weak, or not stupid, to ask for such help.

26.3 How we create anchors by choice

During our NLP training it is explained that through using anchoring we are able to first select a desired state, and then to anchor it so that we can reaccess this state at will. There are obviously hundreds of different states of desirable emotional feeling and, of those, some of the most frequently-suggested states which people wish to anchor are such things as:

a) happiness
b) calmness
c) relaxation
d) love or tenderness
e) motivation

26.4 Problems with anchoring

However, if we think back to one of the structural pre-suppositions of GOLD Counselling, we must remember that it has been stated that:

> *To achieve a goal or feeling or objective, one must first remove the beliefs that are being fulfilled which are exactly 180° in the opposite direction. Rather than add positive thinking, first remove negative thinking.*

If we take this concept a step further, let us, therefore, determine the opposite states to each of those listed above:

a) sadness
b) nervousness
c) tension
d) rejection or coldness
e) lethargy or apathy

What is normally found is that most people know exactly what the positive states are which they wish to anchor, but it is this second list of opposite and limiting states which keep on surfacing within their lives. Using the methodologies embodied within GOLD Counselling it is possible to identify and eliminate the exact root causes of these opposite states, so that the original desired state can then be accessed at will.

If it is true that people have all the resources which they need, then it is through this removal of the limiting anchors which hold us back that we will be able to access those desired states whenever we want. From this position we will then be able to develop additional new experiences which serve to reinforce us as the new person we have become.

26.5 Revised procedures

Within NLP one is taught how to elicit a state and then anchor the related feeling, either to an external cue, such as touching a hand, or an internal cue, such as imagining a particular scene.

We can then use the various anchoring techniques, such as chaining anchors or stacking anchors, in order to develop within the client an even more powerful set of resources. One particular type of technique which is taught within NLP is the means by which individual resourceful states are anchored to different fingers on each hand, permitting these to be accessed at will.

Once you have understood the effect that the underlying negative beliefs will continue to have on your mind while they are still there, it is possible to understand why many anchors, even when set supremely well, will fade in a short time.

However, once you have eliminated the negative beliefs associated with the opposite state to that which you want to anchor, anchoring the new, desired state will be that much more accessible.

Let us take the example of a client who had a problem with not being able to create enough wealth in his life. Specifically, he was not able to move towards money successfully, always finding reasons why something couldn't happen, or why a way of doing something couldn't work. He had spent much time using the techniques set out within personal develop-ment literature and specific NLP techniques but nothing seemed to stay in place for long. While this may have been due to his own approach, we decided to work with him using GOLD Counselling. This revealed under-lying beliefs about always being poor in his childhood, but the belief was continuing to operate in the here and now and was eliminating any possibility of his creating wealth for himself or his family.

Once this set of limiting beliefs was released we then restructured the remaining positive elements and future-paced him towards the success he would have now and this had the effect of creating positive anchors in his mind to create the success which had once eluded him.

27. Circle Of Excellence

This is a very simple and clever technique which can be taught to clients so that they can very quickly and easily align their resourceful states by using a spatial anchor. If we again reconsider the presuppositions contained within Chapter 10, we should naturally assume that there could well be underlying negative beliefs which contain thoughts stopping them from automatically achieving their desired state.

By using the standard framework of the GOLD Counselling language we can identify with the client when it was that he first learned to believe that he was not able to access his desired state.

Let us use the example of a person who is having problems with a lack of confidence. If asked to be more specific he may say the most noticeable situation is one of staying confident while interacting with his superiors. Dealing with this may be a simple matter of revealing when he first felt unconfident when with his superiors.

It would then be appropriate to ask a question such as, *"What do you need to believe to believe that you can be confident in front of your superiors?"* This will cause his unconscious mind to imagine and access the desired state. At this stage, significant changework has already taken place. We could then enhance his confidence further by employing the Circle of Excellence technique, whereby we can identify and add other emotional states, perhaps taking examples of associated feelings he would find useful in his selected situation.

28. Internal Conflict Manager

As practitioners one can be presented with many different types of problems by clients. However, many of these can be chunked up to one of the following two formats:

1. *"Well, I'd really like to be able to do X, but then I feel Y and then just can't."*

or

2. *"Well, I want to stop doing X, but then something stops me."*

From both of these scenarios it is clear that there is some inner disagreement which is taking place within the client's unconscious mind. What we need to be able to do for our client in this situation is enable him to resolve this pulling in opposite directions and align the two (or more) elements for him.

From reference to the pre-suppositions of GOLD Counselling we would expect that there are two or more inappropriately matched and opposing beliefs at the centre of this problem. Following a brief questioning phase with the client, it would be possible to determine whether two separate topic lists need to be constructed, or whether a single map will cover all beliefs, including the opposing beliefs.

Once the GOLD Counselling topic list has been produced and worked through, additional work may continue. One may choose to use the Internal Conflict Manager, where the practitioner can guide the client to firstly separate out each part and secondly determine what beliefs are supported by each part. From this position the practitioner can then have the client negotiate an agreement between the varying parts. This should result in these parts no longer causing the client to be pulled in different directions.

This approach relies on consensus between the parts, therefore all of the parts will still be in place when the technique is completed. Furthermore, any limitations put in place from any of the parts will impact upon and reduce the flexibility of the other parts.

The next step is facilitated by the therapist applying a technique that removes any parts that are found to be no longer of use. Once this occurs, the remaining parts can be integrated in a strong, positive and congruent fashion.

29. Visual-Kinaesthetic Dissociation
(Fast Phobia Cure)

29.1 How phobias are created

As we go through life we are all presented with many different and varied situations. Some of these are pleasant, some are mediocre and some are distinctly unpalatable. Of those which are unpleasant, there are sometimes incidences which are so uncomfortable, so unpalatable that the person experiencing these becomes revolted by the incident. It is at this stage in the mental process that a phobia can become formed. This happens when the unconscious mind takes a single element from the original memory and then whenever this element is experienced, a phobic reaction occurs.

Take the example of a young boy who experiences being locked in a dark room. The incident would be repressed, but the emotional fear that the young boy felt would become attached to the idea of being alone in a dark room. Once this process has occurred the experience becomes lodged as a memory within his unconscious mind. Following this, whenever he is presented with a situation which resembles the original experience (i.e. has the element of the dark room), he suffers anxiety, nausea or fear.

It is an unfortunate fact that many people seem to develop phobias. Quite often people do not recognise that what they have always put down as their *"silly little foible"* is actually a phobic response to something. Our records show that there are over two-hundred recognised phobias and probably many more as yet unnamed versions. In simple terms, there are as many different phobias as there are things to fear or situations to fear.

Many people with phobias have to suffer in silence, rearranging their lives to fit round their phobia, often having the problems with the phobia compounded by well-meaning individuals with their messages of such things as *"pull yourself together"* or *"it's only a little spider"*. Other comments often proffered by clients include such things as, *"but you're a grown-up now"*, or *"that was so long ago"* or *"don't let that bother you"*.

29.2 How phobias grow in strength

The problem with phobias is embodied within one of the most powerful iron laws which is written into the very fabric of all branches of psychology and self-development:

The thing you fear most is the thing you attract.

However, it is an unfortunate fact of life that phobias if left alone do not go away. No. They grow, slowly and surely, debilitating the person with the phobia more and more as time goes on. This means that the person who fears spiders will soon have to start looking in the corners of rooms *just in case* there are any spiders.

To explain this further we shall use an example of someone who was trapped in a lift. After a while he might find that other small rooms may cause him discomfort. Later on he may find the phobia has spread so he does not want to enter office blocks which have lifts. If left untreated, the phobia will later spread to incorporate not wanting to enter buildings *just in case* he has to use the lift in them.

29.3 The pure NLP approach (Bandler, R.,1985)

One of the most used techniques within the NLP Practitioner's tool kit is that of the double-dissociation, or the visual-kinaesthetic dissociation. This can be used to remove phobias which have, until now, stubbornly resisted any attempts at eradication through desensitisation, positive thinking or plain denial.

However, by the time the client presents himself for help, the phobia may well have expanded and changed in many ways. This means that although he may feel he has a phobia towards X, in actual fact, the originating phobia may be Y, something so uncomfortable and from so long ago that he has chosen to forget it totally.

If one were to apply the visual-kinaesthetic dissociation towards the presenting problem, provided that the problem was the original object from which the phobic response was created, the technique could be permanently successful.

However, how would you as the therapist, or how would your client, know that it was the originating cause, especially where one considers that he may have "forgotten" where the original phobia came from? It is because of this substitution effect of the phobic response that the under-lying phobia could well be missed.

29.4 The NLP/GOLD Counselling approach

Nevertheless, if a client were to present himself to you with a phobia and you were to ask him to prepare and work through a GOLD Counselling topic list with you, it would then be possible to determine exactly where the originating memory about the phobia was formed.

Placing information about the beliefs and thoughts related to the phobia is less stressful than having to re-experience all the times when it had been triggered. However, the information collated in this way is very powerful and enables the therapist to use his client's unconscious mind to direct him to the root cause of the problem. This is then worked on directly to eliminate any further incidences of the phobic reaction.

Very often the client will realise during the session that the reason why he had always thought he had his phobia was actually incorrect. Once this confusion is released and the real cause identified, the phobia reduces and dissipates thereafter.

Furthermore, once the phobia has been released the therapist can restruc-ture the client's positive beliefs about the object or situation which produces the phobic response so that he would then be quite ambivalent about the subject.

30. Swish Pattern

The Swish Pattern technique was developed to assist people in stopping unwanted habits by asking their unconscious mind to develop new and more appropriate behaviours to replace them (Bandler, R., 1985). We have found that through introducing GOLD Counselling at an initial stage of the changework, before using the Swish to revise behaviour, a deeper, more permanent change will occur.

This is explained by the fact that the GOLD Counselling analysis enables the client to actually understand, perhaps for the first time ever, where it was that he learned to believe that his habit (e.g. biting nails) was an appropriate way to behave.

We have all been cautioned, when preparing our client for the Swish Pattern, to ensure that he focuses on what he wants in a positive way as a new person, rather than what he doesn't want. For example, if someone's presenting problem was that he bites his nails, we would ask him what he would rather be able to experience. He may well say something such as being successful, having manicured nails and good-quality skin on his hands, or perhaps seeing his hands holding the steering wheel of a powerful motor car. While it would then be possible to carry out a Swish Pattern with this information, the change would not be permanent. This is because no attempt has been made to facilitate in the client the removal of the beliefs that are related to his habit of biting his finger-nails.

Even if we ask him why he does it, he will only be able to answer using his conscious awareness since if he really knew why he continues to bite his fingernails, he would be able to exert his conscious will-power and cease the habit permanently.

What we must do is to generate a GOLD Counselling topic list whose subject matter will be the exact habit which is presented. This analysis will enable the therapist to determine when and where the habit was installed. Following its release, a new and appropriate behaviour can be integrated that will be lasting, since the client will no longer have any resistance to the new habit becoming permanent.

31. New Behaviour Generator Strategies

31.1 Creating new states

So many people, when first introduced to the new behaviour generation techniques are simply amazed by their powerful simplicity (Dilts, R., Grinder, J., Bandler, R., Delozier, J., 1978). Through this technique it is possible for new behaviours and new ways of thinking and acting to be quickly and accurately first modelled and then learned.

This element of NLP practitioner training can have a powerful effect on most participants' lives since it means that they can now generate in an instant new patterns of behaviour.

One of the key tenets of NLP is that all people already have within them all the resources which they need. Even if they have only ever been able to obtain that feeling, perhaps, of success or elation or calmness for just a few seconds, they have experienced it. They already know in both a psychological and a physiological way exactly what the experience is which they want.

So many people don't realise that they do have within them the resources which they need. However, we as therapists need to let them first understand that if they do want a particular state of mind, they must have been able to imagine it or else they wouldn't know whether they had really wanted it originally.

The challenge faced by those same people is that they are not able to, on a consistent and automatic basis, access those feelings which they feel they truly desire. For many varied reasons the same people are finding it difficult or perhaps impossible to access that particular state of emotion freely whenever they deem it appropriate.

31.2 Incorporation of GOLD Counselling

By including the GOLD Counselling approach at a preliminary stage of conducting sessions with the client, it is then possible to confirm where the limiting beliefs were first installed and then to remove them. Once this is completed, reinforcing beliefs can be added to ensure that the new behaviour becomes permanent. At this stage, utilising the New Behaviour Generator and specifically-worded suggestions, using GOLD Counselling language or the Milton model, one can ensure that the client is now fully and concurrently aligned with the beliefs he now seeks.

Let us now use as an example a client who told us the following:

Client: ...*and what I'd really like to do is just tell them what I think, but I don't feel able, or confident enough to do so. Yes. That's what I need, more confidence. Can you help me?*

In this instance we know that from within the framework of GOLD Counselling we would anticipate that one or more of these statements is true:

1. he really does not know how to do what he wants, which is unlikely since he does know what it is that he wants to be able to do

2. he doesn't really feel that he deserves to, should do, can do or such like, due to another, probably hidden, limiting belief

3. he has tried this desired state before, perhaps many times over many years, or perhaps just once, and the feelings associated with that failure were so powerful that further attempts have been precluded

4. his problem is actually a symptom of something else – his mind is letting him focus on this so as to guide him away from the real issue which is out of his conscious awareness

From a cognitive review of these permutations, it is possible to understand that if one were to adhere strictly to the standard New Behaviour Generator without clarifying what is stopping the client from accessing the desired emotions, the positive effect of the technique will soon dissipate. However, by accessing the unconscious mind's information as to the specific beliefs held about that emotional state, it is possible to remove the limitations which currently exist. Once this barrier is removed the client will be able to access his desired state. This could be enhanced further through the existing New Behaviour Generator techniques.

32. Well-Formed Outcomes

If you don't know where you're going, you will probably end up somewhere else.

The journey of a thousand miles begins with but a single step.

If you were to review the various books currently available which discuss success strategies, or motivation theories, or ways to create happiness, you would be able to identify one consistent theme. In addition, if you were to study any of the various schools of psychology, you would find that they all have one issue which they all seem to agree on.

People who are most able to achieve happiness, stay healthy, enjoy life and achieve those things which they really desire, are people who have worked out what they actually want from life.

It therefore follows that these same people have, by inference, also worked out what they don't want from life, such as poverty, sadness, depression or loneliness. Now it may be that they have just focused on what they want, or perhaps ignored what they don't want, but one thing is certain, they know what they desire.

If you were to take a survey of how most people focus on their goals you would find that most people are able to recite the many things which they don't want to happen in their lives but they will often have problems with identifying those things which they do want.

On the occasions when a client presents this problem to a therapist, usually the next steps, as suggested by NLP and other personal development training, is to work with the client to restate what he doesn't want into what he does want. From this position it is then possible to get the client to co-operate with you to develop a congruent well-formed outcome which will move him forward to his newly-desired state or goal. Where this procedural sequence fails is that it does not address the underlying reasons why the person has not achieved his goal in the here and now. Consider again the pre-suppositions of GOLD Counselling in Chapter 10. In this we state that the unconscious mind does not understand the difference between either the past tense and the current tense, or the current tense and the future tense. Therefore, even though you may have been able to develop a supremely well-formed outcome for your client and elicited all the desired states which he needs, you have not removed the original limiting belief which has meant that success has eluded him before now.

It is this original and still-operating limiting belief which will reduce or even eliminate his chances of success. What is unfortunate is that the client will not realise that his old beliefs are still in place and he may return for further assistance to refocus himself on his desired goals. However, by using all your usual NLP and personal development techniques, after incorporating a GOLD Counselling analysis to determine why he has not yet achieved his goals, his success will be that much more assured.

33. Six-Step Reframing

In the same way as it is possible to enhance your successes with the Swish Pattern, GOLD Counselling can also be used to increase the success of the traditional Six-Step Reframe (Bandler, R. & Grinder, J., 1975).

If we take, for example, someone who wants to stop smoking. Using the Six-Step Reframe technique it is possible firstly to identify the positive intention behind his smoking habit and then to utilise his own unconscious mind to develop alternative strategies and new ways of behaving which will fulfil the same purpose. While this technique can and will generate new behaviours, the session can be less successful than it first appears. This is because the client will not realise that the presenting problem – that of not being able to stop smoking – is actually connected to another issue linked at an unconscious level.

We would now always direct our clients to complete a GOLD Counselling topic list on **"Smoking"** which would be worked through before carrying out the Six-Step Reframe. In these instances it is invariably the case that the Six-Step Reframe will either not be required, or will be applied to an entirely different area of that person's map of the world which is the real and underlying issue.

This means that the therapist can apply the appropriate techniques to the appropriate causes of the symptoms and not merely address the symptoms.

As an example, consider someone who wishes to increase his confidence when undertaking public speaking. If we question him further, he may explain that he gets a nervous feeling in his stomach, linked to an increase in perspiration immediately prior to standing up to speak. We ask him to connect with the part responsible for this feeling and by clarifying the positive intention behind this will generate information. However, unless the originating cause that gave rise to this positive intention is removed, it will continue to cause a problem for the client.

This is when the concept of symptom substitution can be experienced. We must assume that a client would not come to us unless he were unable to change his behaviour himself. Accordingly, we must also assume that there is something within him but out of his control and it is this which the Six-Step Reframe identifies.

If we use the analogy of a computer program it is possible to understand with even more clarity the problems of symptom substitution and the effects of "and therapy" when the therapist seeks only to add positive suggestions onto existing beliefs without first addressing the cause. Many of you will have heard of the computer programmer's phrase "garbage in, garbage out" or "GIGO".

However well written a program is, it takes time and energy for this to be run and for an output to be generated, even if it is inappropriate or incorrect. This inappropriate output will continue to be produced even though it is useless, since the program believes it is required.

These problem scenarios are often not identified when the program is first written. Many programs are so complex and contain so many permutations that errors cannot be found until many years after the original programming was carried out. The original program has often been written in a code which is no longer understood and, therefore, cannot be rewritten. This means that a new program has then to be written, running after the first program, compensating for the error, causing additional energy to be expended.

This is the same as "and therapy" where the error is not corrected but covered over, meaning that other problems resulting from the initial error in the original program permeate into other areas. As a result, additional work-around programs will be required to correct further errors when identified. Every one of these will take time and energy to be run, causing the system to run slower and slower by taking up more and more memory.

Taking this into a client situation, this means that he will fabricate more and more procedures, habits and ways of acting to cover up and mitigate the impact of his underlying problem, without ever uncovering where the errant learning had first been written into his life.

Over a period of years a client may unconsciously generate tens or hundreds of small work-around programs, each draining his energy. However, once the original programming has been rewritten, all of these additional programs can be deleted, releasing the associated energy for use in other areas of his life.

Provided we take our client through a GOLD Counselling session which focuses on the habit or problem presented by the client, we will be able to determine exactly where his limiting belief originated. This will ensure that we can rewrite the errant programming instead of adding new programs to cover-up the problem. This simplification of his life will free-up energy and enable him to succeed in a simpler and easier way.

34. Stepping Up And Stepping Down Exercises

34.1 Overview

If you were to ask someone to tell you what is really significantly important to him in his life, you might well receive a response such as to make more money, or to have a bigger house, or to be able to spend more time with his children. If you were to take this as a starting point, you could then ask him to imagine for a moment that he had already achieved this goal. Then ask from that position, what would having achieved this do for him.

Within most styles of personal development and therapy techniques, it is taught that the goals and objectives that we have are in turn connected to other goals and objectives. It therefore follows that by peeling back these layers one by one, the underlying reasons why your client really wants to achieve something can be revealed. This can be best expressed as the difference between *"ends"* and *"means"*. With this approach, the therapist enables the client to convert the *"ends"* (the activity or result that he wants) into a *"means"* (to let the client gain a deeper understanding of what having this would do for him).

34.2 Stepping up

Within NLP there exists a technique known as *chunking up* (Dilts, R., 1990). If we use a simple example, we can explain how the method would be applied. Let us assume that a client has come to see you as a therapist to gain assistance in being able to change his career. In this event, the therapist would use specifically-worded questions such as:

Therapist:　*What do you want as an outcome? (ends)*

Client:　*To be in a good job with a much better income than my present one. (ends)*

Therapist:　*And if you achieved this outcome of being in a good job with a much better income than your present one (ends), what would that do for you? (means)*

Client:　*I would then know that I can provide for my family. (ends)*

Therapist:　*And if you achieved this outcome of knowing that you can provide for your family (ends), what would that do for you? (means)*

Client: I would know that I was successful. (ends)

Therapist: And if you achieved this outcome of knowing that you were successful (ends), what would that do for you? (means)

Client: I would know that I had done good, that my life was good. (ends)

This technique would normally be applied by repeating the steps above until the client reaches a spiritual level, which is usually the deepest most profound state which he can achieve. By recording each of these steps and then taking him back down from this deep state to the original ends from which it was developed, a deeper understanding and focusing on his goals will be generated.

34.3 Stepping down

In addition to this, a technique has been developed which focuses in the opposite direction on the client's barriers to success. This technique is called, naturally enough, stepping down.

Once the outcome has been identified, the first question asked is "What stops you?" Having identified this, the therapist then asks the client "What do you want instead?" Again, once the limitation has been identified, the client is again asked "What stops you?" By taking this exercise forward, stepping down and then down again, it would be possible to understand the real and underlying reason for not achieving the original outcome.

If we were to now revisit the same presenting problem discussed earlier, let us compare how the stepping down process would work.

Therapist: What do you want as an outcome? (ends)

Client: To be in a good job with a much better income than my present one. (ends)

Therapist: And what stops you? (limitations)

Client: I'm not sure what I want to do. (limitations)

Therapist: And what do you want instead? (ends)

Client: To know what I'm good at. (ends)

Therapist: And what stops you? *(limitations)*

Client: *I'm afraid that I can't find anything better to do. (limitations)*

Therapist: And what do you want instead? *(ends)*

Client: *To find a better career. (ends)*

34.4 Problems with these approaches

In this way the client will be directed by the therapist to investigate the inner reaches of his mind in order to ascertain the barriers to his success and then to determine what he would desire instead.

However, both of these techniques carry with them a specific and dangerous flaw in their logic. This flaw is based on the premise that one can use linear logic when dealing with the thought patterns within the unconscious mind. We have found however, that the unconscious mind uses non-logical logic, or fuzzy logic, when processing thoughts and beliefs. If we reconsider the original presenting problem for a moment we can understand this more easily.

Client: *I want to be in a good job with a much better income than my present one.*

If we ask a logical question, we will be given a logical answer. We will then find ourselves drawn away from the deeper, unconscious beliefs which are really impacting on his success. This will happen because the client will not be consciously aware of why he is not achieving his desired goals. The only way to understand this is to map out his unconscious thoughts which make up his beliefs in respect of the subject.

34.5 The GOLD Counselling approach

This information would be revealed simply and concisely if the client were asked to prepare a GOLD Counselling topic list such as:

* My career
* Rewards
* Job satisfaction

From this we would be able to determine exactly where the limiting beliefs are which are stopping the client from achieving success in the present.

35. Reduction In Learning Difficulties

Some of the greatest advances in NLP have related to the techniques developed for use in assisting people with reading difficulties to overcome their problems (Jacobson, S., 1981). For many people who have been assisted by these techniques, the changes which have been effected have been amazing.

It has been shown that many children appear to have problems when first being taught to read, which, if not dealt with appropriately in time, will have become accepted as negative beliefs about their abilities.

Much work can be carried out in trying to help these children (or at a later stage adults) break through the barriers related to their specific learning difficulty. However, we have found that in many instances, the actual blockage to learning – the negative belief – was actually formed before the attempts to learn the particular subject (such as reading words) took place. It is as if these children had learned to believe that they were not good, competent or successful at learning anything as a result of that earlier incidence. Furthermore, although they may have hidden away the pain of the originating cause, the trauma of the original experience is still hanging over their lives like a thick, black cloud and continuing to affect them in the present.

Using GOLD Counselling in conjunction with your existing NLP skills means that it is possible firstly to determine exactly when, where and how your client learned to believe the belief that he can't read, or he doesn't get maths right, or he doesn't like reading out loud. Very often, the belief was formed in a situation, perhaps only indirectly related to the specific subject where the problem now exists. It will, however, have had a profound influence on your client. Once this limiting and negative belief has been removed it is then possible for the therapist to use the wide range of tools which he has to assist his client in becoming the person he desires to be. This will be helped by the fact that the client will now have access to so many more internal resources than before.

Often when a client states that he is, for example, dyslexic, we find that it is a very specific type of dyslexia. With one client, he was managing his own building company and was capable of understanding technical drawings and carrying out mathematical calculations, although he believed he couldn't read or write. The GOLD Counselling session revealed that this belief was specifically focused on words and not numbers. As a result of a sequence of GOLD Counselling sessions, he identified where the repressed discomfort related to learning to read was buried. Once released he had no further problems and was able to continue with the learning which had been abruptly stopped during childhood.

In the same way a client will often believe that he knows he has a learning difficulty whereas he has often actually taken in the beliefs of his teachers or parents. It may, in fact, have been the teachers or parents who really had the learning difficulties. This can be evident in situations whereby a client's parents have had to leave school and earn a wage at an early age. This fact can often be unconsciously communicated to children in the message that they should, in turn, also go out to earn some money. Once the client can identify whose belief this really is, he can then determine whether he wishes to take on further education himself.

36. *Sports Improvement*

Significant improvements can be made to the sports successes of people when the approaches within NLP are applied to their problems. Future Pacing, Circle of Excellence and New Behaviour Generator are three techniques often used. However, we have found that when a person has identified in himself a limitation, we need to assist him in permanently removing this prior to offering any further help.

For example, a client wanted to build more muscle. Regular gym sessions were proving fruitless. A GOLD Counselling list was prepared on the topic "**Weight**". During the session which followed he identified that the top part of his body was, metaphorically, stuck in childhood and only the bottom half had grown up. In the session he identified that the feeling of his torso being small was linked to an occasion when he had been held down on his bed during a traumatic incident with his parents. Furthermore, regular bullying in school had meant that he had learned to believe that he always needed to be a good runner. Releasing these incidents from his mind enabled him to realise the reason why his exercise programme had always been focused on lower body fitness. He was then able to revise this to that which was appropriate for him now.

In the same way, many apparent limitations in respect of sports achievement and success are often found to link back to other apparently unrelated incidences which have occurred in the client's life many years ago. By applying the GOLD Counselling approach it is possible to identify and remove this unconscious limitation.

37. *Habit Elimination Routines*

Many people develop different habits, addictions or routines, certain ways of doing things which – however hard they try – they just cannot stop. These include physical problems such as hair pulling, smoking or overeating but these could just as often be a habit of regularly experiencing a certain limiting feeling, such as guilt or sadness.

In exactly the same way as we know how to be happy from earlier reference experiences which have formed a belief that we can be happy, these various habits which a client develops will have been generated from earlier beliefs formed from earlier experiences.

As a therapist, you must be able to locate the originating reference memories which have formed the client's belief that his habit is an appropriate way to behave. Once this is identified and a new viewpoint formed, the habit will cease. Change is natural and flowing and it is only the unresolved originating cause which is holding back the client's flow forwards with change. It is important to understand that the unconscious mind never does anything without a reason. Therefore, however apparently debilitating or destructive your client's habit is, it exists for a reason and until that reason has been identified and the errant belief revised, the habit will continue.

If a therapist only corrects the habit in the present, the underlying reason will still exist and will seek to generate a fresh habit within the client. However, by applying GOLD Counselling techniques to the underlying presenting problem it is possible to identify and eradicate the desire within your client's unconscious mind to continue with this habitual pattern.

In addition to the specific questions set out within Chapter 15, which reveal how to identify where and when a belief was formed, there are other questions which are specific to determining where habits were first formed.

When did you learn it was appropriate to do (habit)?

What needs to happen for you to begin to believe that (habit) is inappropriate?

By correctly identifying where and when the belief about the habit was first formed, it will be possible to remove from your client the need to continue with this habit any longer.

With some habits, such as eating problems, the underlying issue may be one of poor self-image or a belief about lack of self-worth or underlying guilt. Once this has been revised, the original eating habit will no longer be required and will disappear. Additional NLP techniques can then be applied in order to assist the person to expedite change into the person he wants to become, building on his existing resources.

38. *Thinking Strategies And Negotiation Strategies*

If we put to one side for a moment the idea of past lives and future lives, most people agree on one issue – life is not a dress rehearsal, it's the real thing. If this is true, why then do so many people appear to meander aimlessly through their lives, hoping that things will go the way they want?

Furthermore, we feel that these people are not just wandering through life aimlessly; they are fulfilling their beliefs. Their life appears aimless because they hold a belief which states that they hope things will become better – but not for them. This means that as long as they can keep their faith (religion) they will have their dream fulfilled in another life.

Set yourself up for success, not failure. So many people aspire to achieve greatness in life, but so few realise anything but a small fraction of their goals in the whole of their lifetime.

If one can eliminate the negative beliefs which have been incorporated into the unconscious mind, those which drive our strategies for behaviour, we will be left with only one automatic choice and that is to succeed.

An often-used quote which succinctly expresses this goes as follows:

Most people never plan to fail; they fail to plan.

However, the pre-suppositions within GOLD Counselling show that this statement is actually FALSE. People do plan to fail, it's just that they don't realise it. By this we mean that no-one would do anything which is alien to his beliefs about how he should act or think. Therefore, if what he is doing is unsuccessful, his beliefs – specifically his beliefs about how he should interact with others – have been poorly learned. Perhaps it may be that the strategies that were taught and learned at school are still being applied in his office life. Or it may be that the way he treated his college friends is the way in which he now treats his wife.

This happens because once a belief is installed it is consigned to the automatic processing capabilities of the unconscious mind. If we no longer know it's there, how would we know when we are using it? Furthermore, if we don't know we are operating via a limiting belief, why would we consider changing it for something with more flexibility?

Let us take as an example a client who visits you in order to improve his strategy for financial management. From the initial discussion with him you identify that he appears to apply poorly-thought-out strategies for investment, linked to poor selection criteria. He feels that his approaches are rather hit-or-miss and somewhat erratic. In addition, when he realises that he has made an error, he is reluctant to act on this knowledge thus exacerbating the final financial cost.

It would appear that he would benefit from learning a new strategy with which to make financial decisions. One option would be to show him how to generate in himself the appropriate states of mind, such as a **dreamer** to create ideas, then a **realist** to bring himself back down to earth, followed by a **critic** to analyse and look for errors in logic. This was first developed from modelling Walt Disney and has become known as the Disney Creative Strategy (Dilts, R., 1994).

By applying this he would then be able to control some of his more impulsive and frivolous urges. Furthermore, if he were to read up on other financially-successful people and learn their techniques, we may well expect his situation to improve for a while.

However, if we were to apply the concepts within GOLD Counselling to this presenting problem, we would approach our client's presenting problems quite differently. Starting with pre-suppositions as previously defined, we can assume that for some reason and on some level our client does not believe that he deserves financial success. Furthermore, we would also expect to uncover a contrasting belief which he holds, an opposite, but still held, belief that he does deserve financial success. So he will continue to try to fail and then to try and fail. This, in effect, means that without knowing it he is continuing to fulfil all the primary beliefs at the centre of his belief structure about financial success, good and bad, empowering and limiting.

If we were to assist this client, we would firstly confirm the appropriate topic for him to construct using GOLD Counselling. This might be **"Wealth"**, **"Money"**, **"Income"**, **"Prosperity"** or whatever you as the therapist deem appropriate, based on your analysis of the problem and having listened to the specific language patterns used by him to describe his problem. After this you would ask him to create a list of beliefs on this topic. Once these were connected together, the GOLD Counselling session would be able to highlight the specific and originating memories from which the disparate and opposite viewpoints came. Armed with this information, you could remove these limiting beliefs and then consider teaching the client new and useful strategies for wealth creation.

It is only at this stage in the process that your client would be able to integrate into his unconscious mind permanently the new learning as to the way in which he could improve his financial situation, since from this moment on, the limiting beliefs have now been removed.

39. Reframing

No particular situation or experience has any meaning other than that which we give it. By changing the "frame" that one views the situation through, it is also possible to change the meaning associated with that situation. This happens because in order to live in the world on a day-to-day basis we need to integrate that which our senses are picking up in the here and now with the existing maps of the world which we have already created from our past.

It is from the reference point of these maps that we will experience the world. Some people may see the world as a friendly place and will have reference experiences to reinforce that belief, whereas others will resolutely believe the world to be a dog-eat-dog environment and, again, they will have had experiences to justify that view of the world. We can see only what we believe; everything else is either repressed from conscious awareness or subject to cryptomnesia.

We have all no doubt found that the different reframing techniques are very effective in shifting the understandings of both ourselves and our clients in situations whereby a strictly analytical conversational session would not. Furthermore, we have often found that one insightful reframe, delivered in the right place and at the right time, can create significant change in a person.

But how do you know that the only filter, or frame, through which the person views the world, is the one he is offering to you then? Or how do you know that perhaps the view he feels he has is in itself part of a much bigger issue, encompassing many more issues?

What is really required is a methodology which enables the user to understand what the real issue is which underlies that presented by the client. This is especially important when you consider that the client won't know what the real issue is, since if he did he would not have the negative belief installed any more and the feelings associated would have been dissipated.

Furthermore, the language used by the client when discussing his problem contains many deeper and more significant meanings, ones which are generated by his unconscious mind. To attempt to identify and reframe each of these would require a significant amount of analytical time, even supposing that the appropriate language became apparent.

However, by asking your client to generate a topic list focused on the theme which keeps on causing him problems, it is possible to identify the deeper structure to which the originating cause relates. From this position one can restructure the actual beliefs which are creating the problem, rather than have to reframe the symptom which is appearing in his map of the world (Conceptually, reimprinting is drawn from the work of Konrad Lorenz and his development of the concept of "Imprinting").

40. Neuro-Logical Levels

The unified field of NLP as developed by Robert Dilts enabled us to understand how we can interpret our internal information and how external relationships are sorted. Since this is a holistic model, it also acknowledges that one element (such as our capabilities) can be inter-twined with other levels (such as spiritual values) indicating our overall direction in life.

When working with someone to align his neuro-logical levels, he can often become aware of when, in a particular part of his life, he is living and fulfilling negative and harmful beliefs. It also follows that as a result of aligning his neuro-logical levels, he will be much more congruent and focused within the different areas of his life.

Due to the various influences on our lives, it is possible to have limiting and even harmful imbalances throughout the various levels. Consider someone who believes that he is a successful businessman, with confi-dence and ability to create wealth. If, however, he also held spiritual beliefs, such as "the ends justify the means" or "might is right", he may then believe it is appropriate to do whatever he feels is necessary to succeed, even if this is harmful to others or illegal. This information would be revealed within a GOLD Counselling session and it would be possible to identify when the original learning occurred. Once this belief is changed, a profound realignment would then take place.

By realigning the neuro-logical levels, it is possible to gain a deep align-ment and spiritual balancing. GOLD Counselling can successfully do this by identifying where disharmony in different levels exists and by providing the means to correct them.

If we look at each of the neuro-logical levels in turn, then it is possible to appreciate where such blockages could arise.

1. Spiritual   *"This is my future"*
2. Identity   *"I can't change the way I am"*
3. Beliefs & Values   *"No one cares anyhow"*
4. Capabilities   *"I can't do it"*
5. Behaviour   *"I must work hard"* or *"I have to help people"*
6. Environment   *"I don't deserve a good place to live in"*

By working through using a GOLD Counselling analysis on the blockages which are identified, your client will be able to integrate new learning at a very deep and profound level and ensure that his alignment, once set, will be consistently adhered to, since the opposite beliefs have been removed.

In addition, as a result of this realignment, any negative influence which may attempt to dilute the new quality of his life will be seen for what it is, since the original blockages and blind spots have now been removed.

Section Five:

Specialist Section:
Contributions From
GOLD Counsellors

Sexual Therapy – GOLD, FAST
Dr Anne Curtis

● **Sexual difficulties almost never have a physical cause, or a physical cause** *alone.*

Individuals and couples have often been told by doctors that their sexual problems are due to a particular illness or physical condition. However, doctors are rarely trained to understand the power and influence of the mind and emotions on the way our bodies work either in disease or in distress. Most of the doctors you meet, including many of the so-called experts in the field, know little or nothing about how these important emotional and psychological factors might be affecting either your physical health or your sexual performance and pleasure, so they look for and tell you only about what they believe to be physical causes. Some physical factors do need to be taken into consideration.

We do, for example, need to consume adequate supplies of all the essential nutrients, including plenty of water, to ensure that all systems in the body can function properly. It is possible that a nutritional deficiency might lead to either a physical or an emotional malfunction and that simply redressing this imbalance with adequate supplements can have a significant influence on physical wellbeing and on sexual function and pleasure.

On the other hand, even if an individual has a physical condition, such as a spinal cord injury, diabetes or even a nutritional deficiency, which might have had some physical effect on normal functioning, can you imagine this individual not having feelings and emotions that are also affecting his or her sexual function and pleasure?

Additionally, even when physical elements are involved in some way *the healing power of the mind should never be underestimated.*

● **Sexual difficulties are almost never about sex – or at least not about** *just* **sex.**

It is often easier to suppress and to hide feelings, from ourselves and from others, during almost any other daily activity than it is when we come to having sex. If we are angry with a partner, or even with members of the opposite sex in general, for example, we may be able to avoid or hide the anger even from ourselves, in our working or family relationships, but when it comes to sex, the degree of intimacy involved makes hiding feelings much more difficult.

Can you imagine enthusiastically giving sexual pleasure to your partner when you are feeling angry, irritated, or frustrated? In such circumstances we may have sex and feel unhappy or resentful, or we may find ways to withhold intimacy, by perhaps going to bed earlier or later than our partner, having a headache, being unable to get an erection or developing disabling vaginal soreness, for example. Alternatively we might find ourselves wanting to hurt a sexual partner physically or emotionally.

- **Sex is a very important way of communicating suppressed feelings.**
Anger is not the only hidden feeling revealed through sexual difficulties in this way. Feelings such as fear and sadness when suppressed may also show up as an inability to enjoy sex, or as reluctance to share sexual pleasures.

In order to be able to enjoy an intimate relationship, we need to deal with all the feelings we have suppressed at one time or another in our lives and the experiences and beliefs these feelings are based on. Over the years I have used and developed a combination of techniques to help individuals deal most quickly, most painlessly and most effectively with their suppressed feelings. One of the best combinations I have found is the use of the FAST method I am going to describe here, along with GOLD Counselling and the energy psychologies.

- **In order to deal with our feelings we need to recognise we have them and respect their importance.**
Most people in our society are brought up believing that uncomfortable feelings, such as anger, are 'bad' and to be avoided. Because we fear what might happen if we allow ourselves to own such feelings, we learn to suppress and to hide them even from ourselves. We may be completely unaware when, for example, we are feeling angry, though at times it may still be obvious to others. Perhaps you can remember talking to someone whose face and body language showed they were very angry, while they firmly denied being aware of any angry feelings?

It is important to realise that all uncomfortable feelings are actually 'good' in that they are important messages from the unconscious mind. When our unconscious mind believes something is wrong in our lives it tries to warn us through making us feel uncomfortable. If we ignore these uncomfortable feelings the unconscious mind will attempt to get the important message across in some other way. If we continue to ignore or suppress any uncomfortable feeling, it may become more uncomfortable still, or we may develop some physical symptom or disease.

The FAST Method

I developed the FAST method to help individuals identify and understand the meaning of their uncomfortable feelings, so that they no longer had to suppress or hide from them.

Once in the open, these feelings can be dealt with more easily.

When we know what we are feeling we have a choice about what we can do with the emotions and the beliefs behind them.

FAST stands for the Frightened/Angry/Sad Test

This is how it works.

1. Start by asking yourself:
'Am I feeling *COMPLETELY*, WONDERFULLY good right now?'

If you have a sexual problem it is unlikely you are going to answer "Yes" to this question.

If you are feeling anything other than completely, wonderfully good go on to question 2. Feeling 'OK' is not good enough.

2. For the purposes of this process all uncomfortable feelings can be divided into three categories:

FEELING FRIGHTENED (anxious/nervous/scared/wary etc.)
FEELING ANGRY (cross/irritated/annoyed/jealous/sore/frustrated etc.)
FEELING SAD (depressed/grieved/dejected etc./BEWARE: 'upset' usually means *angry* rather than sad)

It does not matter which particular word you want to use, as long as you recognise which category, or categories, the feeling belongs to.

If, as often happens, you are at first unable to say which category your feeling fits, go through the categories one at a time, writing down what the feelings FRIGHTENED, ANGRY and SAD mean to you. Are they good feelings or bad? What has been your experience of these emotions as a child and as an adult? How were these feelings expressed in your family?

This can help you understand why you may have been avoiding or suppressing these feelings and why you may find them difficult to identify.

Now go on to read my explanations for the meanings of each of these feelings and see how these explanations differ from your own previous understanding.

Frightened

Most of us find it relatively easy to identify feeling frightened, nervous, anxious or apprehensive.

The important first step in dealing with fear is to ask:
   'What is the worst possible thing that could happen for me in this situation?'

Let your imagination have complete freedom, without censorship, because you need to deal with all the worst possible fears, disregarding logic at this stage. If your answer is "I don't know", then ask yourself "If I did know, what would it be?" Or make up a worst possible outcome and work with that.

The most disturbing aspect of fear is often being unclear what the fear is about and therefore feeling powerless. Once you can identify the worst possible threat, you have choices and thus power, which can bring great relief even before you take any action.

Having identified the fears we have three choices for what we can do next. We can:

1. Run away
2. Face up to the perceived threat
3. Get help

There is no 'right' choice for every situation. The choice will depend on the person and on the circumstances, but if we do not identify the fear we cannot identify our choices.

For example, if a rabbit is sitting in the middle of the road and can hear a thundering noise getting louder and louder, it could remain where it is, either until it is run over, *or* until a lorry roars past on the other side of the road, so that it has suffered the terror of getting run over for no reason. On the other hand if this rabbit were able to identify the worst possible outcome, it could appreciate it has three choices; to run away; to face up to the lorry, or to get some help – and it could then establish its own power through making a choice. For the rabbit the best choice may seem obvious. In other circumstances there may be more than one good option. We almost always feel happier, however, when we discover we have a choice and that we therefore have power over what happens to us.

Additionally once the feeling has been identified we can use the other therapy techniques, such as GOLD Counselling, alone or in combination with the energy psychologies, to deal with the discomfort and to eliminate the problem if anxieties still remain.

In the case of a man with a sexual problem who is feeling frightened or anxious in the consultation room, his worst possible fears may be:

1. 'The therapist will think I'm ridiculous and laugh at me.'
2. 'The therapist will tell me I am a hopeless case and my problem will never be resolved.'

Exploring such fears with the individual is often a very useful way to establish or improve rapport and trust.

Andrew, for example, was fearful that I, as the therapist, would laugh at him because he had a sexual problem. I encouraged him to look at his choices in view of this fear. He realised he could choose to leave immediately; he could choose to continue the session and discover whether or not I would laugh, or he could choose to find help perhaps by expressing his fear to me, or by bringing someone else in for support. Having become aware of his choices and having realised he had chosen both to stay and to ask for my help through expressing his fears, he felt less anxious and more in control.

I then suggested he consider how he might feel if the worst possible threat became reality and I did laugh at him. If I laughed he would feel angry, because of the meaning he derived from my behaviour. He believed my laughter would mean that I was not valuing him or his feelings, but he would suppress this anger rather than express it to me because of a further fear. His worst possible outcome now was that I would throw him out if he expressed anger, so that he would lose any chance of ever resolving his difficulty. Again I asked him to consider how he would feel if this worst possible outcome became a reality. He said he would feel angry with me again, because he perceived I would not have respected him or given him what he needed.

By following his feelings through in this way he came to appreciate that expressing his feelings would help him to discover at this early stage whether or not this therapist did respect him, his feelings and his needs, and therefore whether or not he was with the best therapist for him.

If I laughed and he did express his anger, rather than the session ending, we might have come to a better understanding. I might have been able to explain why I had laughed and have understood better what my laughter meant to him, so that we could find a way of working together better. Alternatively, if I had thrown him out, rather than losing his chance, he would have an opportunity to find a better therapist for himself.

This exercise helped him to understand there was nothing to fear and only more to gain by recognising, respecting and expressing his feelings.

Angry

Anger is a very useful and very important emotion, and suppression of anger is a very common cause of sexual difficulties.

Most of us grow up believing anger is a negative, damaging, or socially unacceptable emotion.

We want to be loved and accepted and many of us are afraid we will lose love and acceptance if we show anger. So we learn many ways to suppress angry feelings, all of which actually have negative consequences for us and for our relationships.

- Sometimes we suppress all of our feelings in order not to feel or to show anger. This often results in *lack of energy, depression* or *loss of libido*.

- Sometimes we allow the anger to build up inside as if in a pressure cooker, until it finally bursts out. The anger erupting in this way is usually totally out of proportion to the final provocation. The recipient, or recipients, of the angry outburst are usually children, animals or weaker adults who we do not expect to lose, or persons of little or no consequence to us, such as other drivers, shop assistants or telephone operators, whose love and approval we are not worried about losing.

- Sometimes we turn the anger back against ourselves. We are not so afraid of losing our own love. As a result we inflict ourselves with hurt, guilt or self-blame.

- Sometimes we act in angry ways towards another person or people. We may do this with awareness, for example, you might consciously say to yourself, 'If you won't do this for me, then I won't do that for you'. Or we may act in a similar way without conscious awareness. Impotence is commonly a way of expressing suppressed anger to a partner. It is a way of saying "I'm not going to give you what you want", though the impotent man is often totally unaware of this unconscious motive or even of any feelings of anger.

Anger expressed in these covert ways is damaging. But if anger is recognised and expressed openly it can have both constructive and enriching results.

Anger is the emotional equivalent of physical pain

Physical pain tells us: **'Something is "wrong" with me and I need to do something about it.'**

If I have appendicitis, the pain I feel has the purpose of telling me that my appendix is inflamed and I must do something about it if I am to survive. Even if I am stabbed, the pain I experience is there to tell me I need to look after myself. First I must remove myself from further risk and secondly I must deal with the injury already inflicted. The pain is a message about me for me. The purpose of the pain is not there to tell me to blame, judge or attack the person who stabbed me, but rather is there to aid self-preservation.

Anger being the emotional equivalent of physical pain, also tells you: **'Something is "wrong" for me and I need to do something about it'.**

Again, anger is concerned with self-preservation and survival, both in physical and emotional terms. It is not about blame or retaliation, though that is what most of us have learned to believe.

It is important to remember that even if I am feeling anger in relation to another person, what that person is doing may be "right" for him or her, even if I perceive it as "wrong" for me.

Since losing his job, Harry was having difficulty getting an erection. As a result he was unable to have intercourse with Sally. When Sally told him "it doesn't matter," Harry felt upset (angry). He believed her words meant their sexual relationship did not matter, or that his sexual pleasure was not important to her, or that the great gift he believed he had been giving her previously had been of no consequence to her.

Rather than expressing his anger and explaining the meanings he derived from her words, he suppressed his anger, and as a result felt pain inside. He distanced himself from her more and more, emotionally and physically, fearing further humiliation and disappointment, and unconsciously wanting to punish her by withholding love and contact. The relationship became more and more strained. Sally now felt upset (sad and angry) that he was keeping away from her altogether, believing his actions meant he no longer loved her or found her sexually attractive. She even suspected he was having an affair. She too suppressed her anger rather than expressing her feelings and thoughts to him, but her anger showed in the way she spoke to him and acted towards him. Thus the relationship became increasingly unhappy. If he had expressed his feeling and the meaning he had taken from her words, Harry would have discovered, as he did during their joint FAST therapy, that what Sally actually meant was "I really care about you and don't want to upset you. Our sexual relationship is important to me and intercourse is only part of it, so I don't want to put pressure on you to have intercourse". She had no idea what her words meant to him and she was doing her best to say the 'right' thing.

Once each started to understand the other's feelings and meanings, they were able to come closer again and to start rebuilding their sexual relationship.

On further FAST exploration of his feelings, Harry discovered he felt both sad and angry about the loss of his job, believing he had lost dignity and status, and he was also frightened that Sally would no longer find him attractive since he now saw himself as a 'loser'. Having uncovered these feelings we were able to use GOLD to reach the core beliefs behind the feelings and used a combination of GOLD Counselling and energy psychology methods to help him resolve his negative beliefs about himself. As a result, Harry's problems getting an erection were resolved, and the relationship improved.

Sad

Feeling sad often means we have lost something important to us. The something may be a person, a body part, a possession, a feeling, a pet, or a relationship; it may be something or someone we loved, or it might be something or someone we are glad to be rid of, but it will always be an important enough aspect of our lives that the loss is very noticeable.

It is obvious to most of us that if we have a body part removed surgically the tissues around the wound need time to heal. These tissues need looking after and caring for during the healing process, so that healing takes place fully and completely. When healing is complete you may be left with a scar, but there is no remaining discomfort. If on the other hand you do not look after the wound as it heals, but instead rush back to normal activities ignoring your needs, healing cannot take place completely. The wound may become infected or may open up again, there is likely to be chronic discomfort and normal life and activities are inhibited.

In a similar way, when we experience an emotional loss, we need time for emotional healing. Emotional healing need not take a great deal of time, but if we ignore the loss and go back to life 'pretending' it has not happened the pain and incapacity can persist indefinitely.

Perhaps you have noticed that individuals who have suppressed their sadness when they have lost someone important in their lives may remain chronically unhappy? Others who allow themselves to experience and express their sadness completely and take care of their emotional needs until healing is complete are able to return to life with joy.

Adults are often afraid to cry and to mourn when they lose something or someone important. The feelings may appear so strong they are sometimes afraid they will never stop if they allow themselves to start. Alternatively, they may believe they should put on a brave face for the children or other adults around them. They do not want to look foolish or to be a burden.

Unexpressed sadness following loss can be a cause of sexual difficulties.

However it is also important to remember that whenever we feel sad we are likely to feel angry too, because we rarely like what is happening to us when we are feeling sad. Since it is often more acceptable to be sad than angry we often convince ourselves we are feeling sad when we are actually angry, so always look out for hidden anger when you believe you are feeling sad.

Jane had lost interest in sex completely since having a miscarriage a year previously. She could not understand what was the matter with her. When she used the FAST process she realised she had been very sad about the loss of her baby, but had not felt able to mourn and to cry. It seemed that the miscarriage was a minor event to everyone else around her. They all wanted her to be happy again and told her there would be plenty of time for her to be pregnant again. She felt she was being silly having such strong feelings about a baby which had never really developed and which she had never had in her arms. Having realised the depth of the sadness still remaining unhealed inside her she was able to allow herself to respect that feeling and to mourn for her loss, so that she could heal.

Along with the sadness, however, she also felt very angry with her partner, with the medical staff and with her family who she perceived as having been uncaring about her feelings. In fact David, her partner, had cared a great deal about her feelings and had felt very sad himself too, but he too had felt he ought to suppress his feelings in order to help her. He was frightened of her sadness and so tried his best to make her feel better.

Bringing these feelings out into the open helped Jane and David to repair and improve their relationship.

Make the most of the FAST method in your everyday life

You can use the FAST method to practice identifying your feelings throughout your everyday life

Remember that though anger is least often identified it is probably present to some degree whenever we are feeling uncomfortable feelings, since anger means "I don't like what is happening for me" and, in general, no one likes feeling uncomfortable.

Once the feelings are identified GOLD can easily be used to explore and to change the core beliefs behind the uncomfortable feelings.

Almost all sexual difficulties are based on one or more of these feelings, which is useful to remember if you are feeling stuck as a therapist.

© Dr Anne Curtis, 2000

GOLD And The Energy Psychologies
Dr Anne Curtis

It's easy.

GOLD is a simple tool for getting to the root of emotional and physical difficulties. If you already use one or more of the energy psychologies, as I do, I am sure you will find GOLD saves a great deal of time in dealing with complicated issues. If you have never used the energy psychologies before, I am certain you will find even one of them to be an enormously beneficial addition to your existing tools, and that in using them with the GOLD method you will experience amazing results both for yourself and for others.

The energy psychologies are a group of techniques, mostly very easy to use, which can be used to relieve physical or emotional discomfort of any kind.

I know my last statement may seem difficult to believe – I was more than a little sceptical when I first encountered these techniques – but I, and many other practitioners, have found the statement to be true.

Still, every time I use the energy psychologies I am amazed when (often in a matter of seconds) they work.

Recently I was in the bathroom at my work place, washing my hands. The lady standing next to me was pulling a face and complaining she was in a lot of pain because she had just hit her ankle accidentally with a golf club. I asked if she would like to learn how to get rid of the pain and she replied that she certainly would. We returned to my office and in less than three minutes she had no pain at all. Instead she was laughing in amazement at the 'magic' we had just performed.

A few months ago I visited the stationers to buy some paper. The young lady behind the counter looked pale and unwell and I overheard her tell her colleague about the severe headache she was experiencing. I asked if she would like to be rid of the headache and when she replied she would, I asked if she would mind looking a bit silly in the shop. Since she did not care how silly she looked as long as the headache would go, I took her through a brief tapping sequence and halfway through the sequence her headache vanished completely. As you can imagine she was extremely happy and I was stunned again by the effectiveness of the technique.

The energy psychologies can work in similar ways for emotional pain and discomfort.

When I first dared to use the techniques in my practice I wondered if my clients might run a mile from this crazy doctor, using such peculiar techniques, but I was wrong, and the results have often been spectacular. In fact, my first professional 'subject' was a lady who had come to see me about a relationship problem. She was very upset and cried from the moment she started to tell me her story. She wanted me to tell her how she could change, so that her partner would love her. He was constantly telling her she must change and she was not good enough as she was, but, she told me, she did not know how to change. As far as I could tell, there was nothing to change, but she could not see this possibility and was determined to change to please him. I explained that I had a strange new technique I would like her to try if she was willing. I told her the technique involved tapping on various acupuncture points on her body, rather than using needles as in acupuncture, and that, though I had one or two theories, I could not really tell her how it worked, only that my experience showed that it did. She said that she was very willing to try anything.

I took her through a very basic technique, which I will set out for you in a moment, and within five minutes she was like a different person. She now realised how badly her partner was treating her. She was calm and no longer crying and was determined she knew exactly what to do. Since she had travelled a long way to see me and we still had over an hour of the consultation left, we used the remainder of the time to go over various other self-help techniques she might find helpful, and dealt with various other secondary issues that arose during our conversation. The following week I spoke to her on the telephone. She was very happy, she had 'sorted her relationship out' to her own satisfaction. She did not tell me specifically what she had done, but she assured me that she was still using the techniques I had taught her, and that she would call me again if she needed any further help. I have never heard from her since.

However, emotional disturbances are not so quickly or easily managed. More often there are layers of beliefs and feelings holding the individual back from true contentment. In such cases tapping, which is what most of the energy psychologies involve, might relieve one symptom only to reveal another and then another. Though the energy psychology techniques continue to work with persistence, it can sometimes take a long time to find the core of the problem, and to deal with the problem for good.

This is where GOLD is so useful.

Using the GOLD method it is usually possible to save a great deal of time working on peripheral beliefs and feelings, since dealing with the core belief entails dealing with the peripheral ones at the same time.

Two particular recent cases come to mind.

The first concerned a young lady, a teacher, who complained of difficulties with her breathing. She felt she became short of breath easily when she was sitting quietly marking books, or at other relatively peaceful times. In fact the problem was not only preventing her from sleeping, it was also ruining her social life. She would now avoid being with friends or suffer silently when she was with them, because she would even notice an apparent shortness of breath when she was relaxing, though she was able to hide her difficulty from others. On further discussion it became clear she had 'always' lacked confidence and so never really enjoyed her job. In addition she was married, with two children she loved very much, but she found it impossible to express her love to her husband or to her two daughters.

I am sure you are aware there are many ways to approach issues such as these. Initially I introduced this young lady to a very simple tapping technique, which worked for her on minor aches, but did nothing for the symptoms she presented me with. It seemed likely there was some underlying core issue which could usefully be dealt with, so we started with a GOLD list about breathing. The list led to three primary beliefs, based around:

TIGHT <—> SHORT   FATAL <—> DRASTIC   WEAK <—> WRONG

I used the next part of the GOLD process to help her return to the origin of each of these primary beliefs in turn. Each took her back to similar circumstances, but the feelings she accessed were different in each case. Her mother left when she was very young and she remained with her father who had always been weak and ill in one way or another. The father spent his life complaining about his poor health and always seemed to be in need of caring himself. He seemed totally unable to show love or caring for his daughter. She despised his constant illness, but felt guilty and responsible as well as angry and resentful. She feared becoming like her father and also felt guilty about her father's poor health, which she blamed on her mother and on 'women', and she had also learned to fear death through illness from her father. In addition, as a child she had lived in fear that her father's illness meant that he might die and thus also leave her. She was afraid she would not survive and experienced difficulty with her breathing when she remembered this feeling. At the point when she was beginning to panic with the breathing difficulty it was very useful to take her through the simple tapping sequence she had already learned, not to take her mind off the feeling, but to relieve the underlying emotional cause, so that the breathing difficulty eased. Once she found herself back in control of her breathing and no longer fearing that death was imminent we were able to go through her other primary beliefs and she was able to change those she discovered were unhelpful to her, such as 'women cause men pain and illness if they get close', using GOLD methods.

It was extremely useful for her to be able to use the tapping methods to help her through the most traumatic and difficult of the feelings she encountered. For example, she found it difficult to face her anger towards her mother, without being overcome with guilt. By using the tapping she was able to face all her feelings and then deal with them in turn. When I saw her again a month later she reported she was no longer having problems with her breathing and she was beginning to feel closer to her own family and felt able to start telling them how much they meant to her.

Though it may be more satisfying for the therapist to the know the story behind the feelings and the beliefs, it is not always necessary for either the therapist or the client to unearth the whole story or memory in order for the individual to deal with the primary beliefs and, as a result, to feel happy. If the individual is able to access the important feelings related to the belief, then going through the sequence of tapping may be enough to resolve the issue. In other circumstances, the tapping sequence allows the feelings to be brought to a bearable or non-existent level, so that the issue can then be dealt with using GOLD or other methods.

The second individual I mentioned was a young man who came to me because his anger was becoming destructive to his relationship and his life. The anger had been building up since his girlfriend had moved in with him. One night he had become irrationally angry when she stayed out later than he expected with friends. He convinced himself she was being unfaithful and by the time she arrived home he was in such an angry state he was not able to hear or take in anything she said. They had a massive row and he threw her out. She had been living near by, but had not returned home, for two weeks. He was afraid she was starting to see someone else and that he had lost her. He told me how much he loved her and really wanted to be with her and could not understand why he could not control his anger. At the same time he still suspected her and was determined to protect himself from deceit.

In view of his ambivalence towards his own anger, I started by taking him through the FAST method, so that he understood and was more comfortable with anger as a useful feeling, telling him something about his underlying needs. So that he could be confident he would be able to control any angry feelings that might arise at any time, I then taught him a simple, basic tapping method. At this time he had a pain in his leg from playing football, so I suggested he tap for this pain in order to demonstrate to his mind the power of the technique. The pain disappeared immediately and this helped him to realise he could use the tapping method to control his angry feelings if or when they arose. I then asked him to remember the evening when his girlfriend had stayed out later than he expected, so that he accessed his angry feelings. As he did so I asked him to go through the tapping sequence. We continued in this way, taking him back to the feelings and to any thoughts or beliefs that were able to trigger the anger, and then going through the tapping sequence, until he was no longer feeling anger whatever part of the incident he recalled. By this time he was feeling calm enough to explore the primary beliefs underlying his anger. He discovered that his anger and his underlying fear related to having found his mother in bed with a 'strange' man when he was a teenager.

He had been for counselling in the past to talk through what had happened because he had cut off all communication with his mother at that time and felt uncomfortable about the situation. He believed that having had counselling he had dealt with that part of his life and it was no longer bothering him.

It became clear to him now however that he still had very strong feelings resulting from that incident. He felt his mother had been unfaithful to him as well as to his father and that his mother did not really love him. As he went through these primary beliefs he was able to realise that many of them were either not true, or that they belonged to someone else. Having reframed these beliefs, or returned them to their original owners in his own mind he found he no longer felt angry with his mother and was even able to contemplate a renewal of his relationship with her. At the same time he could now see and experience more clearly the situation with, and his feelings for, his girlfriend, and was able to talk to her about renewing their relationship on a more equitable and trusting basis.

In summary, I find the energy psychologies and the GOLD method a very powerful and useful combination. It is extremely useful and comforting for both therapist and client to have a powerful tool, such as the tapping sequence, at hand to deal quickly and effectively with any feelings that are 'too much' to stay with. At the same time it is wonderful to be able to save time tapping on any and every feeling that arises, by getting to the primary beliefs and related feelings using GOLD.

How to do it

This is one of the very simple tapping techniques I use and you might like to use to relieve or eliminate both physical and emotional discomfort. It is a very basic version of the Emotional Freedom Therapy (EFT), which was developed by Gary Craig from Thought Field Therapy (TFT), the original energy psychology developed by Dr Claghan.

Perhaps you know how effective acupuncture can be. This is very similar, but you will be glad to know that there are no needles involved, and that you can do it yourself.

How to do it

- First decide which uncomfortable feeling you are going to deal with. For example, you have a pain in your shoulder or you are feeling frightened your lover will leave you.

- Write down on a scale from 0 – 10 how strong that feeling is now (e.g. 10 = extremely strong and 3 = mild fear).

- Find the **karate chop point** on the edge of your hand (left hand if you are right-handed or right hand if you are left-handed). This is the point that would come into contact with an object if you were giving the object a karate chop (a point on the edge of your hand halfway between the base of your little finger and your wrist).

- Use the tips of the first two fingers (index finger and middle finger) of your other hand (right hand if you are right-handed and left if you are left-handed) to tap firmly on this karate chop point.

- While you are tapping on this point, say to yourself 3 times: 'even though I am frightened my lover will leave me (or whatever your feeling is, for example, 'even though I have this pain in my shoulder...') I completely love myself. It doesn't matter whether or not you believe what you are saying, whether you feel stupid doing it or whether you believe in what it will work – just do it – what have you got to lose?

- Now use the tips of your first two fingers on each hand to tap on the top of your head 7 – 10 times, then just above the inner tip of each eyebrow 7 – 10 times, then on the bone at the outer edge of each eye 7 – 10 times, then on the bone just under the middle of each eye 7 – 10 times, then halfway between your nose and your upper lip and halfway between your lower lip and your chin 7 – 10 times, then on each side of your upper chest – 3 cm down and 3 cm out from the notch in the bone at the bottom of your throat, then lastly under each arm, directly down from the armpit, about where a bra strap would go round.

- Now assess again how strong that feeling is on a scale from 0 – 10.

- If the feeling is less strong, go through the tapping process again, until the feeling is gone altogether

- If the feeling does not change, you might want to find someone with experience in one of the energy psychologies to help you, or you might ask yourself what the underlying emotional cause might be for this feeling, and then tap for that cause. Take for example the feeling that 'I believe I am too ugly for him/her to love me'. Start the tapping by saying 'even though I believe I am too ugly, I completely love myself' and continue the tapping process. There may be many layers to this feeling. Every time you have dealt with one layer, another might become clear. You might choose to do a GOLD list at this stage to find the primary belief and then tap on that.

- If you are still stuck with the feelings you could choose to find someone who has experience with energy psychologies to help. You can visit my website for resources at

http://www.reallylove.com

or you can contact me through ICET.

Rape And Sexual Abuse
Jacquelyne Morison

A client may arrive in your consulting room with a given set of symptoms which may indicate the possibility of emotional, physical or sexual abuse in childhood.

A client will suffer from the effects of emotional distress when he or she has been or feels physically or emotionally neglected or abandoned in childhood. The loss of a parent's affection, for example, may be registered in the client's mind as neglect or abandonment if a parent dies, leaves home, suffers from a prolonged illness or is simply not interested in the child's progress at school.

A client will suffer from the effects of physical abuse when he or she has been severely punished, strapped, caned, bullied, maliciously attacked or beaten in childhood. The client will suffer, for example, if he or she has been over-harshly maltreated physically within the family circle and then, subsequently, becomes vulnerable to physical bullying at school.

A client will suffer from the effects of sexual abuse when he or she has been ruthlessly exploited for the personal sexual gratification of an adult or adults. The client, for example, may have been a victim of incest, been interfered with by a stranger or a friend of the family and will suffer from the traumatic nature of such assaults on his or her integrity.

The client who has been a victim of childhood abuse will, in general, have been unfairly used and exploited in order to fulfil the emotional needs of an adult or adults at a time when the child was unable to protect him or herself. The effects of such misuse will inevitably take their toll on the client, who may or may not clearly recollect the experiences which led him or her to seek therapeutic assistance. Most clients, of course, and, in particular, childhood-abuse sufferers, will have little or no conscious awareness of what has caused their symptoms, problems or distress, and therefore, the therapist's job will be to provide time and opportunity for this unfolding.

In all cases of childhood abuse, the client will present a range of symptoms which may indicate to the astute therapist where the nub of the problem is likely to reside. Of course, any suspicions on your part, as a therapist, should not, under any circumstances, be voiced to the client. But it is your duty to gently and compassionately lead him or her towards beneficial realisations by providing an opportunity for him or her to unburden him or herself of the trauma, distress and psychic conflict which his or her early experiences have engendered. The victim of childhood abuse, in essence, will suffer from the distress of having been betrayed by an adult or adults when the original abuse occurred and, of course, if the client has suffered as a result of parental abuse, the effects will be even more profound. The betrayal factor is likely to manifest as feelings of sadness, grief, anger and resentment and, in addition, the client may have developed a poor judgment when trusting others in adult life – thus rendering him or herself wide open to further exploitation.

Furthermore, because the child will have been rendered powerless, helpless and unprotected by the abusive experience, he or she may, in adulthood, assume the role of victim. The client is likely to have had no choice or limited choice when the abuse occurred because of his or her overriding instinctual need for dependency on parents, teachers and other adults during childhood and, therefore, he or she may exhibit symptoms and mannerisms indicative of guilt, low self-worth, vulnerability and hypervigilance and the accompanying feelings of impending doom, anxiety and despair.

With victims of childhood sexual molestation, the client will, moreover, suffer from symptoms of sexual traumatisation such as sexual dysfunction, sexual identity-crises, tendencies towards sexual deviation, feelings of sexual inadequacy and/or psychosomatic disorders related to reproductive systems as a direct result of his or her childhood experiences.

The sexually-abused client may also suffer from the effects of stigmatisation whereby a continual feeling of guilt will pervade and control his or her personality, behaviours and interactions with others. A low self-esteem or a self-blaming attitude, for instance, may indicate that the client feels unconsciously responsible in some way for the abuse. Evidence of self-mutilation and substance-abuse are also often symptoms representative of feelings of guilt and shame in connection with this perceived stigma.

The abused client may often not wish to openly discuss aspects of his or her past with a therapist until such time as he or she feels safe in the therapeutic environment and is truly ready to disclose the abuse and to work through the consequences of such disclosure. The therapist, therefore, will need to tread very carefully in such circumstances and to be aware of the fact that any therapeutic intervention may unwittingly unearth memories from the past which have hitherto been pushed aside or even buried in the client's unconscious mind. A compassionate, caring and non-judgmental therapist who has undergone a detailed investigation into his or her own past will be of great benefit to such clients and, in turn, this work offers unparalleled rewards for the dedicated therapist.

A case of rape

Let us now look at an example of a female client who came into therapy as a result of having been raped in adulthood and who was suffering from symptoms indicative of post-traumatic stress disorder. These symptoms included experiencing constant panic, disturbing nightmares, fearful flashbacks to the rape-incident and withdrawing from social interaction which led, eventually, to the breakdown of a relationship with her partner.

The client reported that she had finally sought therapy after her partner had walked out because she had refused to have sexual intercourse with him since being raped. Initially her partner had been supportive and understanding of her need for attention and reassurance, but because of her reluctance to go out socially, he felt that she had crippled his social life and cut him off from his friends. Because of the change in their social life and intimate relations, the client's partner had eventually been unfaithful to her and had then left the communal home – leaving her feeling devastated by the loss, alone, uncared for and unclean. She admitted that the feeling of being unclean was uppermost in her mind and, therefore, the therapist began work in this area.

Topic: *Unclean*

A) I am terrified	**B**
B) I am petrified	**A**
C) I am shaking	B
D) I cannot get away	**J**
E) I cannot struggle or fight because he will shout at me	D
F) I will never be the same again	**G**
G) I feel dirty and contaminated	**F**
H) I feel sick in my stomach	G
I) I cannot wash away my feelings	G
J) There is nowhere and no-one to turn to	**D**
K) I have been let down by everyone	J

Unclean

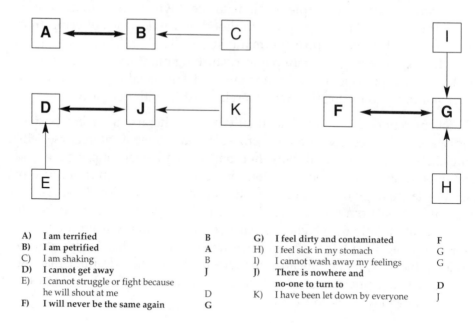

A)	I am terrified	B
B)	I am petrified	A
C)	I am shaking	B
D)	I cannot get away	J
E)	I cannot struggle or fight because he will shout at me	D
F)	I will never be the same again	G

G)	I feel dirty and contaminated	F
H)	I feel sick in my stomach	G
I)	I cannot wash away my feelings	G
J)	There is nowhere and no-one to turn to	D
K)	I have been let down by everyone	J

The GOLD topic list on the subject of feeling unclean revealed that the client had belief loops for:

I am terrified (A) and I am petrified (B)

I will never be the same again (F) and I feel dirty and contaminated (G)

I cannot get away (D) and there is no-one to turn to (J)

As the item G (I feel dirty and contaminated) had the most potency in this belief map, the therapist decided to work with this idea by asking the client where she learned to believe that she was dirty and contaminated.

Client: *I felt dirty and contaminated after I was raped and when my boyfriend finally left me. He just packed his cases and said he was leaving because he felt that I was impossible to live with. He couldn't understand how I was suffering and he didn't even try. Everyone lets me down and goes off.*

Therapist: *Everyone?*

Client: *Yes. My friends let me down, my sister let me down. Everyone!*

Therapist: *Everyone? Anyone else?*

Client: My mum didn't want to know about the rape. She just brushed it aside. She never wanted to know about anything to do with me. When I brought my homework back from school, my mum wouldn't even help me with it. She was a teacher and could easily have helped me. My own teacher was never able to explain to me what I should have done. And so I was stuck. I got told off for not handing my homework in the next day but I didn't know how to do it. When I told my mum about this, she just shrugged her shoulders and walked out of the room saying it was my own fault. Bloody cow!

Therapist: Yeah! Bloody cow!

Client: Yeah and when I told her that that babysitter had showed me his thing, she just said that he couldn't have done that!

The client was then gently invited to reveal any additional information she felt able to share with the therapist about the experience with the babysitter. At this point, the client unburdened her soul with plenty of abreaction. Although her abusive experience was an isolated incident, it transpired that this man was some time later prosecuted for child sexual molestation but that her mother had refused to allow the client, when a teenager, to come forward and to give evidence during the trial. It seemed that the mother had been more concerned with what the neighbours might think than with vindicating her own daughter. The client now began the process of working through issues of betrayal, rejection, guilt and shame.

This case illustrates the fact that a client may present symptoms of one disorder which, in therapy, may actually conceal another ripe for revelation. In this client's case, the rape-trauma had unknowingly triggered her memories of childhood sexual abuse and emotional neglect. The client sought therapy for feelings associated with rape only later to realise that those same feelings of panic, shame and loss were those which she had felt when her mother had not supported her after she had disclosed sexual abuse in childhood. The client explained this situation as follows:

Client: I felt frightened when I was raped but strangely enough I felt even more frightened when I was alone. The rapist just walked out on me after he had raped me, leaving me crying, and this was somehow even more frightening than the actual attack because I was alone with my thoughts. When I saw my boyfriend, I thought he would put it all right by being loving and understanding but, in fact, all he could think about was his friends and what people would say – just like my mother! He was just like my mother who said that the babysitter could never have done that and even when it was proved *that he was a child-abuser, she still didn't believe me. She didn't want to believe me! It was at that time that I first felt dirty and contaminated. It made me feel sick and it made me feel as if there was nothing I could do about it.*

Subsequently the client learned to deal with her feelings from the root source. She vented her anger against her abuser and her mother, she bewailed the loss of her mother's loyalty and protection, she assuaged the feelings of guilt which had accompanied both her rape-incident and the childhood sexual abuse. She was able to relinquish her feelings of being unclean and contaminated because she no longer suffered from feelings of guilt and rejection. The client also realised that she had been a victim of circumstances for most of her life and that the rape-incident was no exception. Working through her feelings of guilt, she was able to relinquish the victim role and to significantly raise her self-esteem. She also realised that she was well rid of her partner and this helped her to overcome her feelings of loss, betrayal and rejection.

Further study

For those therapists who wish to gain a greater understanding of cases of childhood abuse and acquire expertise in this important and rewarding field of work which affects many of our clients (even those who ostensibly exhibit only minor disorders) refer to the *Victims of Childhood Sexual Abuse* course which is run by ICET. This diploma course is for practising and newly-qualified therapists who wish to specialise in treating clients who have been victims of childhood emotional, physical and sexual abuse.

Section Six:

Assignments

Assignments

There are errors in the following examples. Can you spot the errors? All answers appear at the end of this section.

Example 1

A) Glad	B
B) Gay	C
C) Cheerful	F
D) Contented	H
E) Blissful	A
F) Happy	H
G) Blissful	C
H) Happy	F

Example 2

A) Lone	H
B) Desolate	D
C) Lonely	H
D) Deserted	A
E) Rejected	B
F) Isolated	G
G) Left	A
H) Alone	A

Example 3

A) Glad	B
B) Gay	C
C) Cheerful	F
D) Contented	H
E) Blissful	A
F) Peaceful	F
G) Blissful	C
H) Happy	F

Example 4
Topic: Change

A) New	M
B) Difficult	D
C) Necessary	M
D) Painful	G
E) Exciting	A
F) Must	O
G) Slow	P
H) Fast	D
I) Looking	M
J) That's that	C
K) Mother	B
L) Grandmother	B

M) Learning

N) Fun

O) No stand still

P) Got to

Q) Improvement

R) Cycle

S) Fresh

A

E

F

F

C

O

A

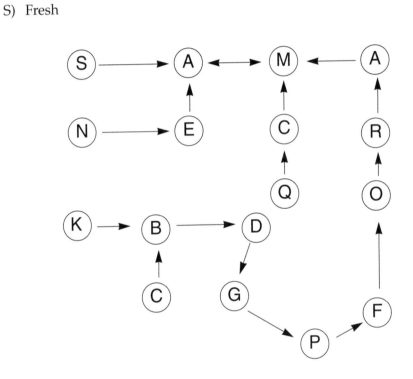

Example 5
Topic: *Change*

A) New	M
B) Difficult	D
C) Necessary	M
D) Painful	G
E) Exciting	A
F) Must	O
G) Slow	P
H) Fast	D
I) Looking	M
J) That's that	C
K) Mother	B
L) Grandmother	B
M) Learning	A
N) Fun	E
O) No stand still	T
P) Got to	F
Q) Improvement	C
R) Cycle	O
S) Fresh	A

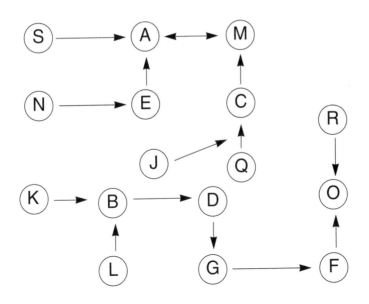

Example 6

A) Happy

B) Laughter

C) Hope

D) Silly

E) Lucky

F) Smart

G) Soppy

H) Stuffy

I) Shifty

J) Smooth

B

A

E

G

C

J

D

I

H

F

Example 7

A) Happy
B

B) Laughter
A D

C) Hope
E

D) Silly
G C

E) Lucky
C

F) Smart
J

G) Soppy
D

H) Stuffy
I

I) Shifty
H

J) Smooth
F

Example 8
Topic: *My Personality*

A) Cool/Calm
E

B) Friendly
J

C) Warm
D

D) Loving
H

E) Caring
L

F) Happy
O

G) Sad
I

H) Giving
L

I) Loner
N

J) Likeable
P

K) Trustworthy   L

L) Honest   M

M) Loyal   E

N) Selfish   I

O) Homely   E

P) Clever   J

Q) Patient   C

Example 9
Topic: Emotions

A)   Happy

B)   Sad

C)   Excited

D)   Peaceful

E)   Lost

F)   Guilty

G)   Frightened

H)   Shy

I)   Betrayed

J)   Motivated

K)   Angry

L)   Alone

M)   Rejected

N)   Elated

O)   Calm

P)   Stuck

Q)   Embarrassed

R)   Loving

S)   Empty

T)   Gullible

U)   Worried

V)   Silly

W)   Grateful

X)   Fragile

Y)   Unaffected

Solutions to assignments

Example 1

In this example you should have noticed that Blissful and Happy are written twice. Remember a word may be written only once. If you were to map out this list you will see that the loop would consist of just Happy flowing to Happy, which sounds good but, in fact, is not appropriate, as you now understand.

Example 2

In this example notice that Lone and Alone are very similar words. You might ask your client if the words mean different things to him. Also notice Lonely in this list. Yes, it is possible to be in a room filled with people and feel lonely or alone but not usually both. Perhaps here you could ask your client to suggest other words or omit either Lone or Alone. Or perhaps ask your client to complete a list on the topic of Lonely or Alone.

Example 3
In this example your attention should be drawn to the word Blissful which has been written twice. Also, in this list, the letter F Peaceful has been linked to itself. Therefore, to map this list would show you no loop.

Example 4
In this example the list and the linking is correct but now notice that incorrect mapping. L, J and H are missing. C is placed in two areas going to B and M. O is going to R and should flow back to F. R should be going to O and not A. A is placed in two areas. Map this list for yourself and find the two loops A and M and F and O.

Example 5
In this example the list stops at S. Notice that O on the list is linked to T yet T does not appear either on the list or on the map. Also H, I and P are missing from the map.

Example 6
In this example notice that A links to B and B links to A. C links to E and E links to C. D links to G and G links to D. This is called pairing. Make it clear that because A links to B that does not automatically mean B links to A. Work with each word individually.

Example 7
In this example letters B and D are linked to two others. One thought can flow only to one other.

Example 8
In this example letter A has two words Cool/Calm. These words should be written separately.

Example 9
This example is for you to link and map for yourself.

Glossary
&
Appendices

Glossary Of NLP Words And Phrases

We have incorporated herein a brief glossary of the specific words and phrases used and defined within NLP. This glossary is intended purely to familiarise therapists who have minimal knowledge of the language of NLP with the important elements of the subject. There are many other books available which go into further detail on each of these subjects.

Anchoring   The process by which a stimulus from an internal or external source causes an automatic change in a person's state. Once set up, whenever the anchor is triggered the linked state will be set off in the person.

"And therapy"   Any therapy which seeks not to correct the cause.

Associated   When one is experiencing or re-experiencing something as if one were actually there. See *Dissociated*.

Auditory   Sensory input related to the sense of hearing.

Calibrating   Using sensory acuity (see, hear, feel) to notice specific changes in a person's external state, and to know when changes are occurring in their internal state.

Capability   The ability to use a particular strategy to carry out an action or sequence of actions.

Chunking   Altering one's perception of a situation or event by shifting up or down or sideways in logical levels. Stepping up occurs when one moves to a level higher than the actual event in order to gain a new understanding. Stepping down occurs when one delves deeper into the event which one is attempting to understand.

Conscious   All that one is aware of, right now.

Deep structure   The underlying linguistic structure which is out of the conscious awareness of the person speaking. This is subject to **distortion, deletion** and **generalisation** prior to any words actually being used to express the deep structure of meaning.

Deletion   The unconscious process whereby one excludes a portion of an experience or a remembered thought.

Dissociated   When one is watching oneself experiencing or re-experiencing something with a consequent loss of intensity of feeling.

Distortion   The unconscious process whereby a current or remembered event is changed to fit one's existing **model of the world.**

Eye-accessing cues   The movements of one's eyes, in regular and identifiable directions, which can indicate what sense one is using to process information. These senses will be either **Visual, Auditory, Kinaesthetic, Olfactory** or **Gustatory.**

First position   Being fully in oneself and experiencing everything from within. Two other **Perceptual Positions** exist – **Second Position** and **Third Position.**

Frame   An outline or body in which a **strategy** can be modelled and then taught to others.

Future Pace   To consider, in the now, how an event could turn out in the future, comparing actually desired results with what appears to be likely to occur.

Generalisation   The unconscious process whereby a single event or a few events are taken to indicate how all similar events will result.

Gustatory   Sensory input or recall related to the sense of taste.

Internal representation   The way in which we all store our thoughts, using the combinations of the five senses.

Kinaesthetic   Sensory input or recall related to our feelings, emotions or touch receptors.

Leading   Smoothly and discreetly amending your behaviour so that your client follows.

Map of reality   The individual and personalised way of experiencing the world which someone has built up, based on how he has experienced or imagined reality in the past.

Meta-model   A model of language and its associated structure which enables the user to identify the underlying meaning of verbal communication which has been **deleted, distorted** or **generalised**. This permits the **deep structure** of the words to be identified.

Milton model   A model of language, exactly the inverse of the **Meta-model,** consisting of artfully vague language structures which overcome the filtering mechanisms within the conscious mind.

Mirroring   Copying the subtle portions of another person's behaviour. See *Pacing* and *Leading*.

Modality   Is a term that references one of the five senses, visual, auditory, kinaesthetic, olfactory and gustatory.

Model of the world   See *Map of reality.*

Modelling   A key NLP process whereby one can elicit the syntax of the ideas or thoughts someone has to achieve a goal. This can then be taught to others.

Neuro-Linguistic Programming   The study of the difference which makes the difference – how different people structure their experiences and achieve their outcomes.

Neuro-logical levels   A model which connects six levels of experience together – **Spiritual**, **Identity**, **Beliefs**, **Capability**, **Behaviour** and **Environment**.

Olfactory   Sensory input or recall related to the sense of smell.

Pacing   Staying in step with another person's behaviours. See *Leading* and *Mirroring.*

Parts	The individual sub-personalities within us, usually with conflicting ideas and behaviours.
Perceptual positions	Our understanding and appreciation of a situation can be from our own perspective (**First Position**) from the perspective of the other person (**Second Position**) or as an observer of the interaction (**Third Position**).
Predicates	The words which people use to unconsciously indicate through which **representational system** they are processing information.
Pre-suppositions	Specific ways of understanding how we interact that must be assumed to be valid so that it is possible to interpret the underlying meanings of these interactions.
Rapport	The act of generating and continuing to have a relationship with someone else whereby the other person feels he is being understood at a deep level.
Reframing	Altering a person's understanding and interpretation of a statement by taking a specific element of that statement and revising it, creating an alternative and previously-unrecognised meaning.
Representational systems	The five different sensory-based organising systems within our minds – **Visual, Auditory, Kinaesthetic, Olfactory** and **Gustatory.**
Resources	A method which one can apply to create an outcome, including such things as physical resources, memories and techniques.
Resourceful state	When one is in a positive, liberating and useful state.
Second position	Understanding an experience from the other person's position. See *First Position* and *Third Position.*

Sensory feedback — The information received from another person through their analogy.

State — How you are feeling or experiencing the world at present. The combination of all your internal and external sensations.

Stepping — See *Chunking.*

Strategy — The specific and repeatable sequence of steps used by someone to achieve a specific outcome.

Sub-modality — Finite distinctions that are applied to our representational systems which affect the way in which we experience and re-experience situations within our minds.

Third position — Experiencing the world from the position of an uninvolved observer. See *First Position* and *Second Position.*

Trance — A state of altered awareness in which one is inwardly focused and able to access memory and imagination at a deeper level than usual.

Unconscious — All that is not within your awareness, right now.

Values — The issues which are important to you.

Visual — Sensory input or recall related to the sense of vision.

Well-formedness criteria — A methodology by which one can design an outcome which is achievable by and acceptable to oneself and one which can be confirmed when it has been achieved.

Appendix I:

A guide to further reading

We trust that after reading this book you will want to incorporate these techniques into the existing skills which you already have. We would suggest that these books will help you to achieve this.

Georges Philips & Tony Jennings: *My Little Book of Meditation*
ICET Ltd., London, UK, 1999. ISBN 0953666719

Georges Philips & Tony Jennings: *My Little Book of Verbal Antidotes*
ICET Ltd., London, UK, 1999. ISBN 0953666700

Georges Philips & Terence Watts: *Rapid Cognitive Therapy*
Crown House Publishing, Wales, 1999. ISBN 1899836373

Richard Bandler & John Grinder: *Frogs into Princes*
Real People Press, Utah, 1990. ISBN 187084503X

Joseph O'Connor & John Seymour: *Introducing NLP*
Thorsons Publishers, London, U.K., 1993. ISBN 1855383446

Anthony Robbins: *Unlimited Power*
Fawcett Book Group, New York, USA, 1987. ISBN 0449902803

Napoleon Hill: *Think and Grow Rich*
Fawcett Book Group, New York, USA, 1996. ISBN 0449911462

Deepak Chopra: *The Way Of The Wizard*
Crown Publishing Group, New York, USA, 1996. ISBN 051770434X

Edward De Bono: *Conflicts: A Better Way to Resolve Them*
Penguin Books Ltd., Middlesex, U.K., 1990. ISBN 0140137777

Robert Dilts with Tim Hallbom & Suzi Smith: *Beliefs, Pathways to Health and Well Being*
Metamorphous Press, Oregon, USA, 1990. ISBN 1555520294

Edward De Bono: *The Mechanism of Mind*
Penguin Books Ltd., Middlesex, U.K. 1969. ISBN 0140137874

Burt Hotchkiss: *Your Owner's Manual*
  Distributed by ICET Ltd., P.O.Box 115, London, N12 9PS. England.
  ISBN 0963536508

David J. Grove & B.I. Panzer: *Resolving Traumatic Memories*
  Irvington Publishers, Inc. New York. ISBN 0829024077

Appendix II

Information on training and joining the Association of GOLD Counsellors.

The Association of GOLD Counsellors (AGC) was inaugurated to ensure that all practitioners trained in GOLD Counselling techniques are assured as competent coaches and tutors. Only registered GOLD Counsellors who have undergone a full and rigorous training themselves are eligible to register as practitioners and trainers and benefit from the Association's referral service.

Within our organisation we offer a selection of training options. These cover all levels according to your current experience and your desired knowledge. Introductory one-day or weekend seminars have been developed so that people with no prior experience of GOLD Counselling are able to learn more about the GOLD Counselling techniques.

Further training exists for practising counsellors and therapists to integrate GOLD Counselling into their existing skills so that they can apply their skills to achieve even more success with their clients. We recommend you attend a workshop if you are intending to utilise GOLD Counselling in your work. Finally, we also have an additional structured training programme for people who wish to go on to become trainers in the GOLD Counselling techniques. This training takes place in recognised colleges, universities and hospitals throughout the United Kingdom and Europe.

Specific training courses have been developed and are run to enable people to take these skills into other arenas such as business and sales development, stress management and the like.

The techniques documented in this book are very powerful and, in consequence, within our organisation we ensure that only qualified and competently-trained individuals are awarded full counsellor or trainer status.

For further details of the full range of training programmes and training materials available, including tapes of our books and training material, please contact the address overleaf.

The Association of GOLD Counsellors
PO Box 115
London
N12 9PS

Telephone no.   020 343 9474
E-mail address   gold@icet.net
Home page   www.icet.net

Training is accredited by the National Council of Psychotherapists.

We look forward to hearing from you and discussing your successes. If you have any comments as to the ideas raised from this book, please feel free to contact us.

The words GOLD Counselling and the GOLD Counselling logo are the registered trademark of G. Philips & L. Buncher ©1997. Unauthorised use is strictly prohibited.

Additional materials available for the GOLD Counsellor

GOLD Modelling Tool software

GMT is a powerful new piece of software created by Ami-software in conjunction with ICET. The GOLD Mapping Tool (GMT) is designed especially for GOLD Counsellors in order to enable them to rapidly generate a clear concise belief map from which to work from. The software like the GOLD Counselling methodology is simple and easy to use. With simplicity of use being a priority, GMT was designed to enable the user to enter the data quickly with minimum number of keystrokes. Once the data is entered the belief map is instantly shown on the screen and the option to print is there. The primary belief loop being the most important part of the map is always easily identified. This tool is a must for anyone wishing to work with GOLD lists regularly. The time saved in mapping the lists is phenomenal, particularly with lists longer than ten words.
Available for Win 95, 98, & NT.
£34.50

The GOLD Psychotherapeutic Counselling Video

This video presentation is designed to accompany the GOLD Counselling book and is intended to demonstrate the use of GOLD Psychotherapeutic Counselling. It is advisable prior to watching this recording to have read, studied and absorbed the principles of GOLD Counselling.
Running time approximately 48 min. VHS format
£25.00

Appendix III

Training courses available from the authors

Certificate in Stress Management Counselling.
A *refreshingly informative* home study program ideally suited for those who wish to take Stress Management to the individual and business community.

Diploma in Clinical & Analytical Hypnotherapy
Probably the most *comprehensive training* currently available. This course is *accredited* by the *National Council of Hypnotherapy* and covers all you will need to know to be a *successful hypnotherapist.*

Diploma in GOLD Counselling
Fast becoming *the psychotherapy of the future.* GOLD Counselling is *a practical psychology* that incorporates *modern diagnostic and restructuring* techniques that have *proven* themselves *invaluable to therapists* in the field of psychotherapy and healing. The course is suitable to only those who are either practising therapists, students of hypnotherapy, psychotherapy, and training or qualified neuro-linguists.

Hypnotherapy Foundation Course
Designed to provide members of the caring profession with an introduction to the *fascinating* subject of *hypnosis* and hypnotherapy. This is a home study course and ideally suited to those who are interested in making hypnotherapy their profession. A great preparation to becoming a hypnotherapist.

Master Practitioner - Gold Creative Psychotherapy (GCP)
Where analysis and repair end, Creative Gold begins. The need to expand, the need to create massive perceptual shifts is vital in the development of new and innovative ways of experiencing life. GCP achieves this using advanced lateral thinking strategies. With structured and focused interventions we are able to alter our perception – the first step in designing and ultimately achieving the life you desire.

Neuro Linguistic Practitioner and Master Practitioner
This course provides an idea opportunity for personal development, achievement and self-fulfilment. The European Foundation of Neuro Linguistic Programmes accredits both courses.

For more information visit us at: www.gtiuk.net

Bibliography

Andreas, C., & Andreas, S., (1989) *Heart of the Mind*, Moab, Utah: Real People Press.

Andreas, S., & Andreas, C., (1987) *Change Your Mind and Keep the Change*, Moab, Utah: Real People Press.

Andreas, S., & Faulkner, C., (1994) *NLP: The New Technology of Achievement*, London: Nicholas Brealey Publishing.

Bandler, R., (1985) *Using Your Brain for a Change*, Moab, Utah: Real People Press.

Bandler, R., & Grinder, J., (1975) *Frogs into Princes*, Moab, Utah: Real People Press.

Bandler, R., & Grinder, J., (1975) *Patterns of the Hypnotic Techniques of Milton H. Erickson, M.D.*, Cupertino, California: Meta Publications.

Bandler, R., & Grinder, J., (1975) *Reframing: Neuro-Linguistic Programming and the Transformation of Meaning*, Moab, Utah: Real People Press.

Bandler, R., & Grinder, J., (1975) *The Structure of Magic Vol. I*, Palo Alto: Science & Behavior Books Inc.

Cameron-Bandler, L., Gordon, D., & Lebeau, M., (1985) *The Emprint Method: A Guide to Reproducing Competence*, Moab, Utah: Real People Press.

Dilts, R., (1990) *Changing Belief Systems with NLP*, Capitola, California: Meta Publications.

Dilts, R., (1994) *Strategies of Genius, Vol 1.*, Capitola, California: Meta Publications.

Dilts, R., Grinder, J., Bandler, R., & DeLozier J., (1978) *Neuro-Linguistic Programming: The Study of the Structure of Subjective Experience, Vol I*, Cupertino, California: Meta Publications.

Grinder, J. & Bandler, R., (1981) *Trance-formations: Neuro-Linguistic Programming and the Structure of Hypnosis*, Moab, Utah: Real People Press.

Hall, E.T., (1959) *The Silent Language*, New York: Doubleday and Co Ltd.

Jacobson, S., (1983) *Meta-cation*, Cupertino, California: Meta Publications.

Jung, C.G., (1969) *Jung Extracts: The Psychology of the Transference*, Boston, Massachusetts: Princeton University Press.

Lankton, S., (1980) *Practical Magic: A Translation of Basic Neuro-Linguistic programming into Clinical Psychotherapy*, Cupertino, California: Meta Publications.

Lewis, B., & Pucelik, F., (1990) *Magic of NLP Demystified: A Pragmatic Guide To Communication & Change*, Portland Oregon: Metamorphous Press.

Index

abreaction, 96, 269
affirmations, 68–69, 75, 117
ageing, 48
analysis, 63, 71–73, 76, 79, 94, 143, 158, 160, 165, 201, 217, 222, 238, 244
anchor(s), 205–207, 209, 285
anchoring, 78, 205–207, 285
and therapy, 224, 227, 285
aspirations, 20
attitudes, 20, 34
awareness, 29, 38, 56, 63, 107, 115, 217, 220, 241, 253, 265, 285, 289

behaviour, 33, 78, 168, 171, 217, 219–220, 223, 233, 237, 243, 251, 286–287
belief(s),
    bridging belief, 111–114
    cell belief, 92
    conflicting belief, 91
    constructive belief, 121
    core belief, 259
    destructive belief, 121
    grafting belief, 114
    harmful belief, 113
    identifying belief, 90–92
    limiting belief, xi, 67, 165, 175, 220, 222, 224, 237
    negative belief, 68, 93, 111, 231, 241
    new belief, 32, 44, 90, 93–94, 115, 117, 119, 121–122, 141
    opposing belief, 39–40, 64, 68, 151, 211
    originating cause belief, 39, 42, 69, 77, 89, 92, 94, 99, 100, 104, 214, 223, 231, 235, 242
    overnight integration belief, 115–116
    positive belief, 67, 93–94, 119
    primary belief(s), vii, 82–83, 91, 97, 101, 107–108, 112, 121, 128, 149, 152, 162, 164, 167, 173, 182, 185–186, 263
    questioning belief, vii, 15, 22, 73, 98, 99, 134, 149, 157–158

restructuring belief, 91–94, 111–113, 115, 119, 129, 295
reworking belief, 101–103
secondary (lower order) belief, 82
source belief, 91–96
useful belief, 113
belief complex, 25
belief cycle, 64, 87, 89, 132, 134, 138
belief list, 78, 82, 129, 133, 138
belief map, 26, 79, 85, 113, 115, 149, 156, 182, 203, 268
belief structure, 9, 23, 25, 29, 31–32, 37–38, 44, 68, 83, 85, 88–90, 94, 96–97, 104, 111, 113, 119, 122, 136, 141, 158, 162, 164, 167, 185–186, 238
belief system(s), 38, 81–82, 87, 117, 119, 121–122, 126, 134

can't, 15, 49–50, 63, 67, 87, 122, 129–132, 134–136, 138, 150, 152, 155–157, 166, 211, 229, 231, 243
change(s), 8, 18–20, 24, 29, 31, 38–39, 42, 49, 56, 61, 64, 68, 71, 76, 78, 87–89, 91–92, 96–97, 99, 101, 115–117, 120, 134, 143, 147, 149, 180, 185, 187, 189, 201, 217, 223, 227, 235–236, 241, 243, 256, 258, 260, 263, 267, 274, 276, 285, 295, 297–298
child(ren), 8–10, 15–17, 21, 24, 32–34, 39, 41, 54, 56, 92, 102–103, 168, 171, 177, 193, 249, 259, 265–266, 269
childhood, 8–9, 15, 17, 38, 77, 96, 159, 167, 169–170, 177, 207, 232–233, 265–266, 269–270
chunking down, 285, 289
chunking up, 211, 227, 285, 289
circle of excellence, 78, 209, 233
communication, 53, 55, 261, 287, 298
complex belief, 93, 94
confidence, 7, 10–11, 22, 69, 209, 220, 223, 243, 259
conscious competence, 33
conscious incompetence, 33

conscious mind, 3, 33–34, 75, 100, 153, 174, 287
consciousness, 11, 57
critic, 238
cryptomnesia, 241
cumulative learning point, 104–105
cyclical, 43

deletion, 24, 285–286
denial, 51, 68, 172, 214
depression, 176–179, 221, 252
desensitisation, 214
design, 44, 117, 120–122, 126, 129, 203, 289
development, 15, 17, 24, 164–165, 207, 221–222, 227, 242, 293
Dilts, Robert, vii, 201, 219, 227, 238, 243, 291, 297
dissecting belief, 98–99
distortion, 24, 285–286
double negatives, 96
dreamer, 238
dual states (multiple states), 29–32

effects, 9, 22, 37, 48–49, 51, 57, 72, 77, 90, 97, 112, 138, 141, 224, 265–266
ego, 18–19, 39, 42, 69, 76, 78, 94, 96, 98–100, 115–116, 130
emotion(s), 48, 89, 91, 97, 103, 219, 252
emotional content, 9, 29, 32, 44, 48, 64, 92, 172
emotional states, 30, 41, 89, 209
energy, 3, 32, 37–41, 43–44, 50, 69, 73, 90, 97, 113, 120, 122, 152, 164, 224–225, 248, 251–252, 254, 257–258, 261–263
Erickson, Milton, 72–73, 297
erroneous associations, 92
expectation(s), 11, 22, 138
experience(s), 7–10, 15, 18–20, 23–24, 29–31, 41, 51–53, 56, 76, 88, 90, 93, 96–98, 100–101, 103–104, 112, 114, 117, 121, 128, 139, 141, 213, 217, 219, 231, 241, 249, 253, 255, 257–258, 261, 263, 266, 269, 286–289, 293, 297

failure, 67, 77–78, 91, 94, 97, 111, 133, 187, 189, 193, 220, 237
fantasy, 8, 12, 21
fast phobia cure, 213
feelings, 7–8, 16, 20, 31, 41, 53, 55, 75, 77, 101–102, 128, 131, 140–141, 155–156, 205, 209, 219–220, 241, 247–256, 258–263, 266–270, 286
filter, 7, 10, 19, 33, 48, 115, 241
filtering mechanism, 31
Freud, Sigmund, 73
Freudian slips, 73
future pacing, 140–141, 233
fuzzy memory, 51

generalisation, 24, 285–286
Gestalt therapy, 63
goal-setting, 68
guilty, 21, 31, 39–40, 103, 149, 180, 193, 259, 279

habit, 11, 115, 201, 217, 223–224, 235–236
habitual patterns, 33

I can't idiom, 129
idea(s), 30, 89, 117, 120, 172, 213, 237, 254, 268
images, 23, 205
imagination, 8, 12, 21, 43, 115, 127–128, 250, 289
imprinting, 242
influence, 18, 24, 48, 69, 75, 89–90, 103, 107, 203, 231, 244, 247
information, 15–17, 19, 23, 26, 29, 33–34, 37, 48, 51, 65, 71, 73, 75, 77–80, 87–89, 94, 96, 99, 105, 108, 115, 122, 133–134, 153, 165, 171, 201, 203, 215, 217, 220, 223, 229, 238, 243, 269, 286, 288–289, 293
inner-child counselling, 63
integration, 37, 115
interpretation, 7–10, 18, 24, 47, 53, 55, 64–65, 89, 98, 288
"is not was" principle, 64